OFFENSE TO REASON

Offense To Reason

A THEOLOGY OF SIN

Bernard Ramm

1817

Harper & Row, Publishers, San Francisco
Cambridge, Hagerstown, New York, Philadelphia
London, Mexico City, São Paulo, Singapore, Sydney

FIRST EDITION

Library of Congress Cataloging in Publication Data

Ramm, Bernard L.
    Offense to reason.

    1. Sin. I. Title.
BT715.R36   1985   241'.3   84–48777
ISBN 0-06-066792-3

85 86 87 88 89 RRD 10 9 8 7 6 5 4 3 2 1

Contents

Original sin is foolishness to men, but it is admitted to be such. You must not then reproach me for the want of reason in this doctrine, since I admit to be without reason. But this foolishness is wiser than all the wisdom of men. . . . For without this, what can we say that man is? His whole state depends on this imperceptible point. And how should it be perceived by his reason, since it is a thing against reason, and since reason, far from finding it out by her own ways, is adverse to it when it is presented to her (445, Brunschvicg).

Blaise Pascal

Preface

Anyone who writes on sin is indebted to Norman Powell Williams's *The Ideas of the Fall and Original Sin: A Historical and Critical Study*. It is a volume of vast learning and rich resource material. However, in many ways it is very dated, for just around the corner from its publication (1929) were two great movements. The first in biblical theology among both Protestant and Roman Catholic scholars who would look at the biblical materials on sin rather differently from Williams. The second movement, broadly known as neo-orthodoxy, would in its own way revive the Augustinian view of sin so distasteful to Williams. In world history also around the corner were the most terrible events of the twentieth century (World War II, the Holocaust, international terrorism, brutal murderous military dictatorships in Africa, Latin America, and The Middle East) all calling for a new assessment of the theology of sin.

We are much indebted to G. C. Berkouwer's volume with the simple title of *Sin*. Here is a brave and learned effort to restate the position of Reformed theology in the light of modern learning but without some of the excesses that have occurred in the history of the doctrine in Reformed theology.

One essay (somewhat dated) summing up the thesis of this work is Lecture 5 ("The Postulate of the Christian View in Regard to the Sin and Disorder of the World") by James Orr in *The Christian View of God and the World as Centering in the Incarnation*. Although sermonic in form, Helmut Thielicke's *How the World Began* contains great insights of a theological nature.

There is not a Greek word or text that I have not traced down in the *Theological Dictionary of the New Testament*. I have referred constantly to biblical encyclopedias and dictionaries, but to avoid excessive documentation, I have not for the most part cited such material.

The German word for Original Sin has a connotation not found in the English. *Erbsünde* has as its root the verb *erben*, which means to inherit, hence inherited sin. This must be kept in mind when discussing German theologians.

1. The Question Posed

Blaise Pascal (1623–1662) was a mathematician, scientist, and inventor. To help his father, who had to spend long hours each night adding up figures, he invented the adding machine. Bothered with the problem of getting around Paris, he invented the concept of public transportation, suggesting that wagons criss-cross Paris on set routes at set times. His seminal thought scribbled haphazardly became, when published, a great book in the history of philosophy and religion.[1]

Speaking of Original Sin Pascal made the following comment: "Certainly nothing jolts us more rudely than this doctrine, and yet, but for the mystery, the most incomprehensible of all, we remain incomprehensible to ourselves."[2] It can be rephrased this way: the doctrine of Original Sin is beyond our ability to explain it, but without it we cannot explain anything. As he wrote, "We remain incomprehensible to ourselves." Was Pascal right?

Apparently the editors of the fifteenth edition of the *Encyclopaedia Britannica* do not agree with Pascal, because they included no entry on sin. The *Encyclopedia of Philosophy* contains no separate entry either but refers the reader to the entry on ethics. Our daily newspapers record the depressing chronicle of crimes but never call them sins. Essays and books recounting some of the most infamous atrocities in the history of the human race do not name them sins. The daily television newscast will occasionally warn us that what is about to be shown might be terrifying for some people, but the terrifying deed is not called sin.

Pascal was no ordinary observer of the human scene. The German philosopher, Ernst Cassirer (1874–1945), gives much attention to Pascal in his work surveying the Enlightenment.[3] It was Pascal who posed the problem of Original Sin for both his generation and succeeding ones. Not only did his immediate successors react violently to him but, as we shall show in chapter 2, the questions Pascal raised are yet much debated. If Pascal was right, then we are all systematically deceived. We are like the human race prior to the development of microbiology. We are suffering from severe illnesses and infections, and we have not the slightest notion of what causes them.

Apart from works on Christian theology and preaching the word sin has dropped out of common discourse. One reason is that the word has suffered an inflation of meanings. Another more important reason is that a secularized culture and a secularized educational system avoid theological terms. If a person wishes to carry on a thoughtful and responsible discussion of the great disorders and fracturings of the personal psyche and corporate humanity, what term does one use? After paging through thesauruses with their lists of synonyms about human evils, the word sin still survives as the best word. For all its limitations, the word sin best describes evils in human experience.

By sin we mean the sum of all the litanies of human woes, evils, and sufferings. Sin means the tragic fracturing that can happen to the human psyche as well as the tragic fracturings in the life of a nation and those superfracturings in international relationships. The litany of sin includes crimes, wars, lawsuits, and mental disorders. It includes all forms of alienation, brutality, and discrimination in our society. It also includes those more polite and subtle ways humans abuse each other. It denotes family problems, national problems, and international problems. It includes personal vices and the vices of governments. Sin is contradiction; sin is violence; sin is serpentine subtlety. Sin is moral inertia; sin is inhuman response to tragic human suffering.

Understood in this context (a broader one than texts on Christian theology and Sunday morning sermons), can there be a more important topic for human discussion? Due to sin (as comprehensibly understood) our judicial system is jammed; our penitentiaries are overcrowded; our police forces overworked. Every school system must wrestle with disobedience, violence on school grounds, and the use of narcotics. Every family feels threatened by disintegration from within or without. War disturbs national and international life.

The concept of sin is not limited to Christian theology. Every work on ethics presumes unethical behavior, which is but a synonym for sin. All great philosophers wrestle with the problem of evil, and sin is a subdivision of evil. All the world's religions presume something is amiss with the human species, and the Christian word for it is sin.

Furthermore, no human life can stand ultimate scrutiny. Antigonus of Macedonia wrote, "The slave who looks after my chamber pot does not consider me a god." This is the ancestral origin of Michel de Montaigne's (1533–1592) remark that "No man is a hero to his own valet." It is well known in the study of sainthood that saints have profound feelings of unworthiness. Those who are close to the bright angels know how sordid human life is.

Pascal further pointed out that sinful humanity cannot see itself clearly. Are we angels or brutes? Are we naked apes or creatures in the image of God? Is the dogmatist or the skeptic right? Is the materialist or the idealist right? Are human beings giants in the presence of a microbe or microbes from the perspective of the stars? We are both the scum and the glory of the universe, but how much is scum and how much is glory?

Philip H. Rhinelander wrote a book entitled *Is Man Incomprehensible to Man?*[4] He examined all the definitions of humanity as distinct from the animal kingdom. Was it art? religion? thinking? toolmaking? But of course he did not discuss sinfulness! Pascal said that humanity is incomprehensible to itself for, being sinners, we have lost all objective perspectives on ourselves. The rest of this volume could be called a commentary on Pascal's problem.

II

No one questions the presence of disorders in society, the evil doings of the professional criminal, the endless warfare among nations, or the corrupt practices of some politicians. The question is whether the Christian doctrine of sin still best explains such evils. The Christian explanation has lost its hold in western society in part because another group of concepts has emerged, effectively replacing or greatly weakening traditional Christian doctrine.

One such concept is conditioning. This means more than a digestive tract automatically starting to function at the sight of food. Rather, it refers to the more general kind of conditioning each person receives from family, community, and even the larger society. We are what we are as the sum of such larger processes of conditioning. Applied to deviant or antisocial behavior it means that factors and forces in the family and community pushed a person in that direction. Causal connections are drawn between deviant behavior and early family life or between delinquency and the surrounding community or peer group.

That there is such conditioning would be foolish to deny. The effect of this concept depends on how much importance we give to it and in what perspective we view it. Heavy reliance on conditioning as a category of explanation results in seeing people more as victims than as agents, more as determined than free, more as pawns than initiators. The criminal, delinquent, or neurotic becomes far more the recipient of surrounding forces than the creator of personal destiny. This all may be true in the larger vision of cosmic sin, but in the range of individual ethics it significantly lessens personal responsibility.

Another concept used to explain moral phenomena is that of mores or social customs. Human societies generate systems of right and wrong actions called mores, and sin is nothing more or less than going contrary to accepted social mores. Edward Westermarck (1862–1939) was a Finnish sociologist, philosopher and anthropologist who made his mark in the history of ethics at two points. He declared that it was impossible to either find or prove a basic minimum ethical code which served as a moral guide to humanity. He further declared that all ethical judgments were expressions of emotions and not rationally determined, which implied that morality was not really a moral code but the customs or mores of a people. If Westermarck was right then of course there is no sin, for sin means at the very least deviation from a norm. Yet according to Westermarck there are only mores and not norms.

A more subtle way of explaining moral phenomena is more philosophically oriented. This view claims that all events in the universe are neutral—they are just there. That the sun rises in the morning is neither good nor bad—it is neutral; it is just there. But human beings have subjective states of feelings which they impose on these neutral events. Moral interpretations are therefore only subjective personal additives. A moral conviction may be a disguised command ("you ought to do this"), a disguised exhortation ("let us all not lie"), or an emotional response ("would that all people loved each other"). In this understanding of moral experience, sin is somebody's subjective judgment on experience. This is really a refinement of Westermarck's theory. If events are not right or wrong in themselves then no actions are sinful in themselves.[5]

The contemporary loss of a sense of transcendence has contributed to the loss of vitality of the Christian concept of sin. By the transcendental is meant the belief that in addition to our ordinary experiences, other overarching realities surround daily life and give it meaning, importance, or even reverence. "Our Father who art in heaven" refers to a transcendental person. That the rules of logic pervade the universe and cannot be violated is a transcendental concept. That within ordinary history a special sacred history works out its purposes is another. The idea of a cluster of moral principles (natural law) by which that all must abide if there is to be social order is also a transcendental concept.

In recent centuries, philosophers and the larger circle of intellectuals and worldy sophisticates have tended to deny transcendentals. The world is as we experience it, they say, nothing more, nothing less. The philosophical term for a world view shorn of every shred of the transcendental is nominalism.

If the nominalistic premise is right, then sin is no longer a meaningful category, for sin can be defined only in transcendental terms. Sin defined as any violation of the law or dereliction of duty places it within a transcendental frame of reference. The denial of the transcendental results again in reducing sin to a breach in mores, to a legal offense (i.e., a crime), or simply to bad etiquette (or as the British say, bad form).

The development of the science of psychiatry has done much to undermine the traditional concept of sin. Psychiatry recognizes healthy, problem-solving behavior or unhealthy, neurotic, problem-creating behavior, but not sinful behavior. It defines behavior as adaptive or nonadaptive, but again not as sinful. A client may be comfortable or uncomfortable in some sexual act, but the person must not add the category of sin to such situations.

It is a popular belief in the counseling community that the category of sin damages people by increasing their sense of unearned guilt. Psychiatrist M. Scott Peck observes in his book *The Road Less Traveled* that the problems churches create in their parishioners sends him enough clients to make an adequate living. He also observes that many psychiatrists and psychotherapists consider religion the Enemy (cap is his) in that religion seems to be such a prevalent source of neuroses.[6] This may or may not be true, but there is no question that psychiatric explanations of deviant behavior have made material inroads on the Christian explanation of sin.

A relativistic or conventionalist interpretation of law also has undermined the Christian doctrine of sin. Western legal tradition carried deep within it both the Hebrew and Roman conviction that human law is a reflection, albeit imperfect, of divine justice. In the Middle Ages a book of law commonly began with the Ten Commandments. Sir William Blackstone (1723–1780) was one of the most important persons to the development of English law, especially common law. His *Commentaries on the Laws of England* formed the foundation of British and American common law. He professed great indebtedness to the laws and ordinances of Holy Scriptures in the writing of his *Commentaries*.

But an interpretation of law that conceives of laws only as rules whereby masses of people in government, industry, and business can live together in relative order is very contrary to the previous notion of law as a system of justice. Law conceived only as a system of social controls continues to weaken the connection between human and divine law, thus also weakening the concept of sin.

The pressures of groups arguing for more sexual permissiveness and fewer ordinances about sexual behavior even further erode the Blackstonian version of law and with that the concept of sin. This new mood of permissiveness is a very complex sociological, cultural and psychological phenomenon. It is not our intention to explore it but only to state that the net effect of it is another instance of the erosion of Blackstone's assumptions.

III

In his great pioneering work on the theology of sin, Julius Müller brought together the problem of sin and the problem of evil. The problem of evil is the larger realm including the cosmic dimensions of evil such as such as natural catastrophes. But the core of the problem is the same for evil as for sin because both deal with something that ought not to exist in the creation of a powerful, wise, and loving Creator.[7]

There is no answer to the question of the origin of either sin or evil if by "answer" we mean a definitive theological or philosophical statement upon which there is common agreement. We can speak only of many attempted answers such as those surveyed in John Hick's (formerly a professor of Oxford, but now associated with the Claremont Schools) book, *Evil and the God of Love*.[8] With reference to such an immense topic we can make only a few observations.

1. Christian theologians have tried to avoid dualism. They have not tried to solve the problem by postulating opposing and independent eternal sources of Good and Evil.

2. They have also tried to avoid a monism in which evil is a means of promoting good. In monism evil is not an irrational destructive force but part of the mix resulting in the larger good of the universe. This view of evil is usually found in pantheisms (world views identifying God with the universe).

3. A traditional view of the origin of evil attributes it to an angelic fall. This view is based on biblical texts such as Isa. 14:3-23, Ezek. 28:1–19, 2 Pet. 2:4 and Jude 6. It has been immortalized in poetry by John Milton's *Paradise Lost*. It explains human sin as

yielding to the temptation of Satan. But it only pushes the problem of evil one step further back.

4. The most common argument for the origin of human sin is that God took a risk. In order to create a full autonomous person in the true divine image that person had to have freedom. But genuine freedom must include the option of disobedience, and in the risk humanity chose to exercise the power to disobey. None have argued more persuasively for this interpretation than the English theologian Andrew Fairbairn (1838-1912) in his work, *The Philosophy of the Christian Religion.*[9]

5. A more recent stance asserts that evil and sin are at heart irrational. They are things that ought not be. Hence they form a logical absurdity, an impossible conundrum. Evil and sin are givens; they have a hard, even brutal, reality. Yet no effort should be made to explain them, for if they could be explained they would become rational and thus lose their essence as evil and sin. Karl Barth provides one example of this way of thinking when he speaks of *Nothingness* (stark reality neither intended nor willed by God). Nothingness is a concept used by such existentialist philosophers as Heidegger and Sartre, and Barth wishes to differentiate his view from theirs. A few scholars see in Barth's concept of Nothingness a retreat to Plato's doctrine of *meon*—the stuff out of which all things are made but which paradoxically resists and accepts the ideal form impressed upon it.

Anyone reflecting on the great evils and sins of our times cannot but suffer some depression of spirit. C. Gustav Jung wrote:

> We stand perplexed and stupified before the phenomena of Naziism or Bolshevism because we know nothing about man. . . . We stand face to face with the terrible questions of evil and do not even know what is before us, let alone what is against us.[11]

Those are the phenomena we seek to discuss and hope to clarify in the following pages. In the following discussion we shall use the expression many times "the historic view" or historic "version of sin." By these expressions we mean that basic set of convictions about sin that the Eastern Church, the Roman Catholic Church, and the churches of the Reformation agree to. In much of this discussion, the debate is more about details such as the degree of depravity or the measure of damage done to the human psyche or the *Imago Dei*. My suggested list is as follows: (i) the human race fell or deviated from its creator at the beginning of history; (ii) that this primal sin caused a major apostasy from God; (iii) that sin works its effects both in the interior of the human psyche and exteriorly in relations with other human beings; (iv) that it incurs the displeasure of God; (v) that as particular people and as a race we are fallen hence sinful persons; (vi) and that the only hope of the fallen race is the reconciling and atoning work of Jesus Christ.

2. If Adam Didn't, Who Did?

The historic Christian doctrine of sin professes to be able to account for the miserable history of humanity from the most violent personal sins to international war. Because the human race deviated from the rule of its Creator, it opened itself to every kind of depravity. However, at the time of the Enlightenment the doctrine of the Fall along with Original Sin and Total Depravity were rejected. European intellectuals as a class repudiated the Christian faith, at least in its historic orthodox forms of either Roman Catholicism or Protestantism. And with that renunciation the historic doctrine of sin fell into disfavor.

However, the phenomena accounted for by the Christian doctrine of sin still remained. There were still crimes, wars, alienation in families, and major group clashes in society. The same miserable history of the human species continued.

In his book, *The Philosophy of the Enlightenment* Ernst Cassirer (1874–1945) notes that, having dismissed the Christian doctrine of sin, many thinkers then cast around for a secular version of Eden, Fall, and Depravity. If Adam didn't, who did? If there were no innocent pair at the headwaters of human history who defected from their Lord and began the miseries of human history, who did start it?

Anticipations of a secular version of sin and depravity appear already in the seventeenth century in the writings of Thomas Hobbes (1588–1679). Hobbes had not yet fully rejected orthodox Christianity, for he did believe that Jesus was the Christ. But there was a secular twist to his doctrine of humanity. His famous definition of human life as "solitary, poor, nasty, brutish, and short" describes human existence in very depressing terms. He assumed that humanity is by nature greedy, sensuous, aggressive, and competitive, seeking war rather than peace. If human nature is lustful, concupiscible, covetous, irrational, and greedy, then it follows that human history will be full of miseries, wars, sufferings, and crimes. This would then constitute a secularized version of the doctrine of sin.

It is difficult to ascertain how much Christian theology remained in Hobbes's system. Many classified him as a deist.[1] He did distinguish sharply between Christianity, which informs us of the kingdom of God, and philosophy, which rests on its own powers of reasoning. Apparently Hobbes derived his view of humanity from philosophy rather than Scripture, so his version of the misery of the human condition is a secular one. This stance of Hobbes is difficult to assess as he was in a period of radical transition. There is some of the old and some of the new in his system. All the bad things that Hobbes said about the human race can be found in Holy Scripture, so in that sense he is saying nothing new. But when he roots his interpretation of the race in philosophical considerations he is doing something new. He is giving a philosophical interpretation of that which has historically been given by theologians. Since his version of the misery and depravity of the race is determined philosophically and not biblically, it is a secular version. Hobbes did speculate about happier peoples like Native Americans—thus faintly anticipating Rousseau—but otherwise his view of humanity appears as a simple given and therefore a naturalistic version of the origin of sin.[2]

Baruch (Benedict) Spinoza (1632–1677) wrote in the same century as Hobbes and promoted his version of the origin of human sin (although he would never use the word sin). Spinoza's philosophy follows a trail in human experience from earliest sensory impressions to the final stage of happiness, the intellectual love of God. The human person has a natural impulse to be free from pain and to seek pleasure or happiness. At root he or she is—in later language—a driven person (*conatus*). But in this drive towards happiness there is a pathway from confused thinking to fully clarified ideas. A person following the route of the clarification of ideas will find happiness. A person guided by unclear or indistinct ideas will encounter trouble. As a creature of drives (*conatus*) the human person is also a creature of emotions, some of them very powerful. Making decisions from indistinct or unclear ideas leads one to stumble into bad emotions like avarice, regret, jealousy, rivalry, anger, remorse, and revenge. Hence those things we call sins or crimes find their ultimate root in the failure of the mind to clarify its ideas—a very rationalistic version of human perversity.[3]

In some ways Spinoza anticipated later thought. His concept of the human person driven resembled Freud's. Certainly his idea that good and evil reside not in themselves but in our interpretations of them suggests the notion of neutral events. Further, he anticipated modern psychology by providing a purely psychological explanation of the origin of human misery and crime.

Although Hobbes and Spinoza were pioneers in proposing secular explanations of human evil, neither developed a systematic theory. That task remained for the next century.

II

François-Marie Arouet de Voltaire (1694–1778) was greatly disturbed by the opinions of Pascal about Original Sin and humankind's depravity. Voltaire sensed that if Pascal were right he was very wrong. He agreed with the stark realism in which Pascal painted the human condition. He could not agree with Pascal's doctrine of Original Sin nor Pascal's belief that we are caught mercilessly between faith and skepticism. He did not think that the gloomy view of the human condition must totally preoccupy our vision.

Two interpretations of Voltaire are possible. Either he did not have sufficient moral stature to fully grasp the problem of sin set out so powerfully in Pascal's *Thoughts*, or else he did not have the philosophical depth to offer a profound metaphysical interpretation of evil or sin. So we are offered no interpretation about evil or sin. In fact his *Candide*[4] was a violent attack upon Gottfried Leibniz's (1646–1716) effort to provide such a metaphysical basis.[5] Voltaire simply asserted that evils and sins are present as part of the mix of life and the universe. In truth, all of the instances of depravity Pascal mentions are really commentaries on the richness and diversity of human personality. Evil and sin are simply posited; they are—in philosophical language—givens.

When Voltaire ended *Candide* with the advice to cultivate one's garden he was saying in effect that we are to refrain from theological and metaphysical explanations. We are to limit our vision to the range of our own powers and our own situation. Perhaps in the future we will find a resolution to the enigmas of evil and sin, but until then we must abstain from speculations.

There is a touch of logical positivism of the Vienna Circle in Voltaire when he affirms that the human mind is incapable of solving great metaphysical riddles. But on the other hand evil and sin are such pressing factors in human existence that reflection about them will not be stilled.

When Voltaire was questioned about meeting his Maker he made his famous sarcastic reply that forgiving sins is God's expertise—*c'est son métier*, "that is what he is an expert about" or "that is his trade specialty." That is how seriously he did not take the matter of personal sin.

III

Scholars agree that the first conscious effort to work out a secular version of Eden, Fall, and Depravity was made by Jean-Jacques Rousseau (1712–1778). Blaise Pascal had written some very strong lines about sin, which Rousseau read and was impressed by them. Having been both a Roman Catholic and a Protestant, Rousseau to some degree understood the Christian tradition with reference to sin. But as a child of the Enlightenment, he repudiated the Christian version of humankind's miseries.

By chance he read that the Academy of Dijon was offering a prize for an essay on the theme of whether advancement and progress improved manners or corrupted them. The mood of the times suggested that the more learning, progress, and science, the better for the human species. Rousseau took just the opposite interpretation and won the prize (*Discourse on the Sciences and Arts*, 1750). Later he wrote another essay for a contest, and, although he did not win the prize, the essay became famous (*Discourse on the Origin and the Foundations of Inequality Among Men*, 1755).

The theses of these two essays were not totally original but they did come as a surprise. When optimism and progress expressed the attitude of the day, it was shocking for somebody to challenge them. It was almost heretical to affirm that science and learning were corrupting France and not leading France to more glory and more progress.

Rousseau created his own original scenario. He had no empirical evidence for his happy savage, but it must be kept in mind that by this time in European history books were being written about the lives and cultures of primitives around the world. In fact, Rousseau asserted that his theory did not need an empirical basis. He intuited that a human person not influenced by forces of corruption was an innocent, happy person—*l'homme naturel*. Outside forces impinged on this proposed innocent, happy society. In Rousseau's limited understanding of economics he picked out wheat and iron as the sources of pressure on the human race. These forces caused society to restructure itself and in so doing created artificial class distinctions among people. A society organized to handle wheat and iron and their pressures becomes compulsory. For example, there need to be craftsmen to deal with those problems created by wheat and iron. From such divisions in society emerges the artificial person—*l'homme artificiel*. Out of these inequalities and pressures and artificial distinctions emerge all the crimes of society, or in theological language, sins.

The secular version of sin is now in place. Eden is the natural person in innocence and happiness. The Serpent is wheat and iron, which introduce the element of temptation. The Fall and Original Sin are the breakup of society into classes and the emergence of the artificial person. Depravity is the sum of all those things produced by the Fall. Now humanity is burdened with endless cycles of alienation that produce the endless crimes, oppressions, and evils of human civilization.[6]

IV

One of the greatest Western philosophical minds was that of Immanuel Kant (1724–1804). He never wandered more than forty miles from his birthplace his entire life yet he encompassed the universe in his philosophy. The most parochial of all philosophers was also the most universal.

One of his great works was *The Critique of Practical Reason*, containing the heart of his ethical system.[7] The great Augustine once asked God to proclaim to him his will, and then give him the will to do it. Or, "I ought but I can't." Kant reversed this notion in his ethical thinking and stated, "If I ought, I can."

Even though Kant moved narrowly between house and lecture hall, he was aware of the full range of human experience. He knew of murder and theft, of treachery and frauds. He knew that a human being was not a pure or simple ethical creature making theoretical decisions in life. Something deeply disturbed human beings so that they as a matter of fact and record did very depraved things.

Kant was not an orthodox Christian. Along with all the other children of the Enlightenment he rejected any and all versions of orthodox Christianity. It was common knowledge that when Kant was in the academic process entering the local church to hear the dean's annual sermon, he would jump out of line at the last moment and make his escape around the side of the church. It is then obvious that Kant could not return to any traditional doctrine of sin or depravity to solve the problems of evil and sin in his ethical writings. In his *Religion within the Limits of Reason Alone* he introduced a section which in the German reads: "Von der Einwohnung des bösen Princips neben dem Guten, oder, Über das radikale Böse in der menschlichen Natur," or, "Of the indwelling of the evil principle next to the good, or, about the radical evil in human nature."[8]

Kant knew that depravity was universal in the human race, for he had read reports of peoples in his days called savages. He also believed that sin or evil is not a definitive part of the human person. So he was caught. He could not find the principle of indwelling of evil in a historical Fall; and he could not find it in essential human nature. So where does it come from? He approached the solution from two different angles. His first explanation posited three phases in the process of growing up from children to adults: a phase of weakness where we recognize the moral imperative but because of our sensual nature we cannot respond; a second phase of impurity wherein we obey moral law from secondary motives; and a third phase of depravity wherein sinful principles have the same rule in a person as moral principles. In modern terminology he explained the principle of evil in terms of the psychology of human growth or development.

The second explanation is very sophisticated and is based on the technicalities of Kant's philosophy. It would not add to the argument of the book nor the clarity of the issues to attempt to recount Kant's more philosophical and abstract doctrine of the origin of evil and sin in persons. It involves Kant's sophisticated distinction between the phenomenal self and the noumenal sense in which he located the ultimate origin of sin in people.

The significance of Kant is his attempt to account for evil and depravity by purely philosophical reasoning. It is, then, a secular version of sin. However, a number of theologians have commented on the seriousness with which Kant discussed the problem of sin. Emil Brunner writes that "Kant's idea of radical evil remains the most serious attempt ever made by any philosopher—who does not bring his system into conformity with the Christian revelation—about evil."[9]

The great poet Johann von Goethe (1749–1832) was on the contrary, unhappy with Kant's doctrine of radical evil in human nature. He said that Kant stained his philosopher's robe (the ancient Greek philosophers wore a special robe) in the doctrine of radical evil so that the Christians would kiss the hem of his garment.

V

The German philosopher Georg Hegel (1770–1831) proposed a comprehensive philosophical theory of evolution before Charles

Darwin suggested a biological one. His scheme of the evolution of *Geist* (Mind, Spirit) was one of the grandest in the history of philosophy. It centered in the development of the different branches of human culture (art, religion, politics, philosophy) and presumed they each had the shape of an ever upward-moving spiral. Each point on the spiral higher than previous points was *Geist* coming to a fuller clarification. In this upward spiraling there had to be critical transition points where lower elements were caught up and reconciled in a higher synthesis. Hegel used the German verb *aufheben* (heave up) to indicate this process of elevating something to a higher level and thus accomplishing a new and higher synthesis.

This spiral pattern applies to human moral and religious development. Persons on an upward moral spiral must at one time have been premoral or innocent. (Animals are premoral and forever fixed in innocence.) The premoral state is not a virtue or a good but a fault or lack. The person who can do only simple arithmetic is excluded from doing problems in calculus, and thus simple arithmetic is a lack, a fault. Persons must cross the threshold from innocence to moral conscience. But this transition is known only through a sense of guilt; and guilt is known only in sin. Therefore sinning is a necessary event in moving from innocence to a mature moral consciousness.

Humankind is differentiated from animals through possessing a moral consciousness. By sinning, humanity made the transition from the premoral state of innocence to moral consciousness. In effect, humanity fell upward. Hegel agreed with Kant that Gen. 3 could be accepted if interpreted symbolically or mythologically, but in his system the Fall of Gen. 3 moved up the spiral. To develop moral conscience, Adam and Eve had to eat the apple.

This view of sin received a good hearing among some theologians of liberal Christianity. Insofar as they too rejected the historic doctrines of the Fall, Original Sin, and Depravity, they needed a theory of human sinning to account for the blatant facts of human depravity. Hegel gave them a model suggesting a new doctrine that would fit into their liberal theology.

Hegel is also the philosopher who took the concept of alienation and made it into a major philosophical category. In the twentieth century it became an important word in existentialism, psychiatry, sociology, and Marxist ideology.

Hegel could also speak of sin essentially as selfishness. If a person was aware of the upward spiraling of Mind that was taking all of culture in its sweep, then not to join in this upward spiraling was an act of consummate selfishness.

VI

Karl Marx (1818–1883) lived at the end of his years in London and in much poverty. Daily he found his way to the public reading room of the British Museum in order to write *Das Kapital*. What a contrast his life presents with the current success of his ideas in such vast countries as Russia and China! If Jesus Christ divided the history of the old world into two parts, certainly Karl Marx has divided the recent world in two.

Readers of Marx have found in his work great similarities to Christian apocalypticism as well as to the Christian doctrine of the Fall.[10] Both Marx and Engels had studied Rousseau's concept of the happy savage's Fall into a structured society. Their own view of the Fall modified Rousseau's view along the sharp lines of economic theory. The proposed original society was a communal one in which each person worked only as much as was necessary for survival. Hence there were no conflicts. One day one of these original persons stepped out of line and produced more than was needed. Marx calls this the *primary accumulation,* and as such it is the Fall and the end of the first communal Garden of Eden. From that Fall came the next great evil. Humankind divided into two classes, and from that division emerge all the ills of the human race. This notion of class division as the source of all human woe is based on Marx's very articulate theory of society and class.

At this point Marx picks up Hegel's concept of alienation. Division into the classes of capitalists and workers creates a twofold alienation. First of all workers are alienated from their work. That which they produce is taken from them and marketed by capitalists who gain for themselves the surplus value of the product. Secondly, the classes are alienated from each other, for now they have become the exploiters and the exploited. Hence alienation virtually becomes a synonym for depravity.

All the evils, crimes, and so-called sins of the human race are now attributed to the Fall from the Eden of the first communal society into the class-polarized world of capitalism. Capitalism in turn produces its own special kind of sin, rationalization. Naturally the capitalists do not wish to surrender their goods and status. They not only protect themselves by police forces and armies, but also ideologically, that is, by the very way they think. A touch of Freud appears in all of this. Marx did not have in mind primarily works that obviously defend capitalism. He thought rather that books on philosophy or religion or politics or economics would be unconscious defenses of the status quo. Of course the outright defenses of capitalism are also part of the ideological warfare waged by capitalists against the workers.

The cure for alienation due to capitalism, in Marx's view, is not religion. If the Fall was economic then the cure must be economic, namely, Marx's version of a truly socialistic economy. Sins, crimes, injustices, and exploitation will disappear if the right economic situation is introduced. Hence the element of Utopia in Marxist thought.

However, in recent years many have realized that some crime can be traced not to economic factors but to neurosis and psychosis in people. Not all sins stem from economic maladjustments. So to class conflict as the source of woes must be added Freud's theories that account for crimes done by mentally disturbed people.

VII

When Sigmund Freud (1856–1939) began his medical practice, treating neurotic patients by hypnosis was very popular and had achieved some remarkable cures. Freud moved away from hypnosis to a method known as ventilation or free association. Stretched out on Freud's famous couch, his patients would ramble on and on—about 700 or 800 hours for the full treatment—expecting something to pop up that would reveal the problem submerged in the unconscious. Listening to his patients going through this process of free association, along with the theoretical issues it posed, led Freud finally to formulate his theory of neurosis.

Freud decided that it was not the Marxian conflict of classes in Vienna that caused neurosis in his patients; the cause was traumatic childhood experiences. Something psychologically damaging had been done in their childhood. By the automatic process of repression it was pushed into the unconscious (for it was too painful to consciously endure); but then something in adult life reactivated the childhood trauma. The adults did not know what was bothering them; that had been effectively repressed. But the symptoms appeared in anxiety and depression.

Freud added two refinements to his theory of childhood trauma. One was his famous triad of the id (the source of drives, appetites, conation), the superego (vaguely corresponding to conscience), and the ego (our acceptable social behavior). If one part of this trio waged war with another part, neurotic symptoms would occur. His second refinement was to identify stages of psychosexual development in children. The first was the oral stage connected with the experience of nursing at the mother's breast. Next came the anal stage associated with bowel movement control (potty training). The third was the genital stage, when the child learns of sexual differentiation. If undue pressures appeared in any of these stages fixation resulted, which in turn would produce neurotic behavior in the adult.

Freud further postulated that the unconscious with its repressed materials was always hammering away rather actively on our consciousness. When it was able to penetrate the protective shield the person committed what is called a Freudian slip.

One kind of childhood experience became central in Freud's thought. It was the *ménage à trois* of the little boy, the father, and the mother. The little boy loves the mother. But he fears the competitor, his father. That which he fears most is that his father may castrate him. But that is a terrible thought; and furthermore he also needs his father. So his psyche automatically represses that thought, but the boy pays a price of guilt and anxiety. When something in his adult life disturbs the psyche the young man will have anxiety attacks and not have any idea of the cause. Freud studied and loved the classics, so he called this the Oedipus Complex (and for girls, the Electra Complex).[11]

As Thelen (professor of Religion, Hollins College, Virginia) points out, Freud expressed himself on this both historically and psychologically. Historically he postulated a primal group very similar to the group used by both Rousseau and Marx. In Freud's tribe or pilot group the young men sought to kill their fathers, acting out a tribal Oedipus Complex. This primal event became the source of the Oedipal Complexes that boys suffer in their personal experience. Freud's point is that our human miseries stem from neurosis. The neurosis is not so much the Fall in the biblical analogy but the *status corruptionis*—state of corruption—of traditional theology.

All human beings are neurotically driven. The symptoms may be modified but not cured, but each person takes neurosis to the grave. When Freud was asked to say a good word about the future of humankind he would not. He could offer no consolation for the future of humanity.·. . Here we have then a secular, psychoanalytic version of Fall, Original Sin, and Depravity.[13]

VIII

B. F. Skinner's (b. 1904) little book, *Beyond Freedom and Dignity* is nothing short of a gospel tract.[14] He paints a most depressing picture of the present situation of the human race. We are facing terrifying problems; and the world appears to be moving towards an inexhorable catastrophe. The lines read as if taken from some apocalyptic, evangelistic sermon. The reason for such doom is that while in physics, chemistry, and biology rigorous experimentalism prevails, the human race is still following outmoded mentalistic psychology. Certain assumptions in that mentalistic psychology both aggravate the situation and render us helpless to stop the impending catastrophe.

Skinner does not postulate a pilot tribe as Rousseau, Marx and Freud did. Nor does he give us any materials with which to postulate his version of Eden and a Fall. That kind of thinking is out of court for Skinner, a dedicated behaviorist in whose hagiography occur such saints as John Watson, Ivan Pavlov, and Bertrand Russell. But we can deduce the identity of the first sinner—the person who started to describe human behavior in mentalistic terms.

The problem with mentalistic psychology is that it assumes that persons are capable of autonomous (free will) acts for which they may be rewarded if good and punished if bad. However, the result is that in our society there is far more punishment than rewarding. The major method of behaviorial control is through punishment or aversive (avoidance) methods. Parents punish children; teachers punish students; the police and the courts punish criminals; nations punish each other in wars. Punishment as a means of controlling behavior backfires; it does not produce the expected result of changing bad behavior into acceptable behavior. Punishment may reinforce bad behavior or create another form of bad behavior (such as a child lying to avoid a spanking). All our evils are then due to mentalistic psychology. To use theological language, we are sinners when we attempt to control behavior through punishment, for we only manage to create more evils.

Skinner also has a gospel, the good news of controlling behavior through the science of technological behaviorism. If we model psychology strictly after the sciences, then all the evils that adhere to mentalistic psychology will disappear. The human race will solve its problems the right and successful way. The gospel is that properly modifying the environment will modify behavior. Operant conditioning, (controlling behavior by reward and not punishment) will save human nature.

Skinner's answer to the question, then, "If Adam didn't, who did?" is obviously mentalistic psychology. Depravity is controlling behavior by punishment. Salvation means repenting from mentalistic psychology and following Skinner's technological, scientific, behavioristic psychology.[15]

IX

Edward O. Wilson would deny that any mention of sin appears in his massive work, *Sociobiology*.[16] Yet such a monumental work cannot go unnoticed, for in theory it proposes that all the social sciences will find genetics to be the bedrock from which theoretical reconstruction is to be done. Sociobiology is defined as "the systematic study of the biological basis of all social behavior" (p. 4). As innocent as that short line appears, it is in reality revolutionary. Anthropology, sociology, and psychology have been built on the assumption that about ninety-nine percent of our behavior is learned from the conditioning of the external environment. Wilson reverses this thesis. He suggests that scientists start with a possible genetic root of behavior. In other words, before we ask if behavior is learned we ought to ask first if it could possibly be genetically inherited.

Wilson's basic assumption is the neo-Darwinian theory of evolution that he calls the Modern Synthesis. However, the rootscience is genetics. This is the meaning of evolution. Therefore all sciences of life must take as their point of departure the science of genetics, for it is our genes that make us what we are. Those creatures that survive have the right adaptive genes and the most fundamental of all genes is the gene of altruism. The altrustic gene means that although animals may devour each other they do not eat members of their own family. This altruistic gene literally leads to the formulation of families (schools, flocks, herds, prides, and so forth). Such families have high survival value. Wilson believes that other factors influence animal behavior—and human too—but we look first for a genetic answer and if we cannot find one, we look elsewhere.

Wilson starts his book with Camus's famous assertion that the most fundamental issue of life is whether or not one should commit suicide. Wilson accuses Camus of talking nonsense. Emotions stem from the hypothalmus and the limbic system of the brain.

When Camus thinks of suicide the brain secretes (my verb) emotions of altruism and guilt, and the suicidal thought is arrested. In Wilson's system the brain actually initiates emotions like hate, love, guilt, and fear, and until we know otherwise we ought to presume that this is part of our genetic inheritance.

Wilson is a learned man. It is remarkable that such a professional biologist both begins and ends his volume with reference to Camus—a Nobel Prize winner in literature. Wilson reads newspapers and watches television news, so he knows the daily reporting of human infamy and depravity. In his book he observes that the human species (as far as its recorded history is concerned) is at war forty-eight percent of the time. Now if Adam didn't, who did?

According to Wilson, our mixed up genetic heritage is the culprit. If Adam didn't, the genes do. Our gene pool is not pure, for "many of the most valued qualities are linked genetically to more obsolete destructive ones" (p. 575). Behaviorial patterns that helped us survive in the past now only work destruction. Of course, the idea that our depravity is a residue of our animal ancestry is not new; attributing it to our genetic heritage is. Altruistic desire to live with peace in one's group may exist side by side with hostility towards strangers. A creative artist may at the same time will to dominate fellow human beings. Parents who nurture children may also have urges to punish them. Wilson calls it destructive behavior; others would call it crime, and theologians would call it sin. It is another secular attempt to account for the miserable history of our species and its current sordid record.

Wilson offers no gospel as Skinner did. His critics think they read in his theory a very definite and unwelcome gospel, the gospel of eugenics. Those with a terribly mixed genetic heritage that makes them destructive people would be eliminated; those with a healthy genetic heritage would be favored. Wilson vigorously denies that his sociobiology has any such political overtones.[17]

X

Ernest Becker stands virtually alone in isolating the problem of evil within the human species and attempting to come to terms with it.[18] Whereas other writers presume evil, none make it a fundamental category and seek to unravel its nature as Becker does. As a result, Becker has written a book that comes far closer to the Christian doctrine of sin than any we have reviewed. The title of the book ought to be *No Escape from Evil*.

In the preface Becker admits that during his lifetime he has avoided looking at "truly vicious human behavior" (p. xvii), that he has fought for a dozen years "against admitting the dark side of human nature" (p. xviii). But he knows that as a scientist he must keep his descriptions accurate. If the human person is a vicious organism, then a scientist will face it, admit it, and attempt to account for it.

Becker's position is very different from Rousseau's or Marx's or Skinner's and, I would presume, Wilson's sociobiology. He many times compliments Rousseau for having been the first person to significantly raise the question of evil in human society and that from a secular, not Christian, motivation. But Becker is very radical in his own way. He writes as if he was offering a synthesis of Marx and Freud, yet very little Marx appears, and much of Marx is criticized. His basic thesis is that humankind as a species, human cultures, and human history can best be explained by the categories of psychoanalytic psychology. Although this is implicitly Freudian it is not pure Freud. He looks to Freud's co-worker Otto Rank for many of his basic insights. More specifically, he takes cues from anthropologists working from a psychoanalytic viewpoint, especially Norman O. Brown.

Becker's thesis means that anthropology, sociology, political science, and economics as customarily treated in university lectures and textbooks are woefully inadequate. They describe symptoms without treating the cause. It implies that each of these specialties is a special branch of psychoanalytic theory. For example, in economic history, money has been considered sacred. Attempting to explain money-matters (economics) on very traditional bases leads nowhere, for until the sacred dimension of money is exposed, the explanation is bound to be superficial.

Becker assumes that human beings have two fundamental appetites: the appetite for food and the appetite for immortality. Our stomachs send us on an endless hunt for food; our powers of symbolization drive us to thoughts or ideas about transcending the persistent demands of the stomach. In short, we are both consuming organisms and creatures endowed with a psychic apparatus described by Freud. Animals too forever search for stomach material, but, having only elementary intelligence, they do not dream up schemes like humans do. Humanity is driven by all those fearsome unconscious powers discussed by Freud and the various symbols, schemes, signs, tokens, rituals, etc., made in response to these powerful psychic pressures. This drivenness breeds evil; it is in fact the source of evil.

Accordingly, Becker rejects all those pilot schemes of a happy natural primitive (Rousseau, Marx, and others who presume a natural state of innocence) and affirms that humanity was evil from the start. We have no record but an evil one. In Becker's scheme, the Fall took place when some human being thought up an ideology or ritual to give the assurance of surviving the stomach! Human beings fell when they tried to latch onto a promise of immortality.

Becker's book is filled with illustrations of his thesis that human beings are driven, neurotic, ritualistic, and symbolizing creatures. The book is one sustained attack against the Enlightenment view of humanity, reason, and progress. Theologically it could be said that the devil and the demonic evicted from academia at the time of the Enlightenment are now brought back into stage center under the guise of psychoanalytic terminology.

The book is very pessimistic, as Becker himself admits. Inner psychic pressures push people toward wrong solutions. If we could cut off these psychic pressures we would suffer no evil. Instead we develop schemes to counter the inner pressures, and they always make matters worse; they are always evil. We think up a scheme to counter evil, but it evolves into a bigger evil. Further efforts succeed only in creating even larger evils. Becker's pessimism recalls that of Freud, who thought all human beings neurotic and refused to provide hope for the future propects of the race.

Further, Becker asserts that the human race has never invented a military weapon it has not used. He does not say the world will end in a nuclear war, but he certainly implies it. If the race always uses its weapons; if the sheer mountain of corpses has never cooled militaristic ambitions; and if our solutions to evil only lead to more evil, then what conclusion can we draw but nuclear holocaust?

In summary, *Escape from Evil* is a secular commentary on the Augustinian doctrine of sin. Although the entire work uses psychoanalytic vocabulary, it translates easily into very standard Augustinian terminology.

Becker admits that his conclusion is purely pessimistic. He then asks if we are permanently stuck in pessimism. He offers three tiny rays of hope: (1) Because we now know our psychoanalytic psychology, we at least know why we perpetrate evil. The mystery of iniquity is cleared up. (2) He envisions in fantasy a group of psychoanalytic experts acting as a kind of remedial leaven in society showing us why we perpetrate evil and teaching us that problems may be solved in the motif of happiness rather than evil. He even imagines being rocketed away to another planet to start over again, but he is not sure this is possible. (3) Finally, if Marxism made such great gains for the poor of the earth, then perhaps Freudian thought, if given an equally massive reception, could introduce enough reason into the human scene to save it from destruction.

XI

Stephan L. Chorover is a modern professor of psychology at M.I.T. in the center of Bostonian sophistication. His book *From Genesis to Genocide*, deals with the ancient Augustine-Pelagius controversy. This ancient debate was essentially a debate about an optomistic interpretation of humanity (Pelagius) and a pessimistic interpretation of humanity (Augustine). It was also a clash of two different personality types. Pelagius was the moral-minded monk who wanted to elevate the spirituality of the monks. Augustine was a typical young Roman citizen who participated in the wicked pastimes of the Romans. The debate is long over but the symbolism of the debate is ever reoccuring. Chorover sides with Pelagius. After giving the pith of Pelagius's opinions he writes: "On all of these points, Pelagius seems to me to be both clear and correct."[19]

But when Chorover gets down to specific cases in the remainder of the book he is actually giving us examples for an Augustinian interpretation of humanity rather than a Pelagian one. Some of his cases leave the reader in a state of shock, such as performing experimental brain surgery that results in the destruction of the self, ego, or psyche of the patient.

This long list of (in many instances very wicked) sinners does not consist of criminal types but rather scientists. They are psychologists, psychiatrists, medical doctors, surgeons, or educators. Most are professors in very important schools such as Harvard, Stanford, and leading German universities. In other words, where we would expect learning, culture, and scientific research to moderate the deeper passions of the human heart we find some of the most barbarous of sinful activities. This is an Augustinian, not a Pelagian, landscape.

The subtitle of the book is *The Meaning of Human Nature and the Power of Behavior Control.* It reflects his basic concern that science (especially psychology) carried on as a very proper, nonideological discipline ("the meaning of human nature") conflicts with political and economic powers in society that insist in meddling in science for its own self-protection. This meddling by "power structures" occasions so much human sin.

Chorover's scenario of a pilot community reconstructed à la Rousseau looks something like this: In a happy primitive community everyone moved freely without intimidation from others. The Fall happened when one person or group organized the primal power play. It decided to control the behavior of the rest of the tribe in order to control the best fishing spot, banana market or other primary good of the tribe. Furthermore, the controlled part of the tribe would be told that this power play was for their own good; it would wear a humanitarian mask. With the power play accomplished and part of the tribe subjected to behavior control, the tribe was thus polarized into classes of the powerful and the powerless.

Total depravity is then the grimy history of humanity in which the smaller power clique is forever controlling the larger powerless masses. With the advent of science, the power play became increasingly worse (a touch of Rousseau here), for science literally is power, and the power of science can be turned to the most gruesome exercise of control. Chorover cites the example of 6,200 sterilizations done in the state of California during the heyday of the Human Betterment Foundation (p. 45).

The demonology in Chorover's book centers on the power brokers. In the case of Galileo, churchmen feared their loss of power over the masses if the pure voice of science were heared and respected. In other cases politicians promote proposed scientific policies (such as euthanasia) to help keep them in power. In other instances business tycoons suppress minorities in the name of science for economic reasons. Perhaps most wicked are scientists who use their supposed scientific expertise and impressive reputations to advocate policies amounting to unvarnished power plays against minorities or the powerless masses. The evil is aggravated when these scientists also hold political office.

Of all the scientific power brokers, sociobiologists receive the brunt of Chorover's judgment. He is a Jew who lost many relatives by reason of Nazi extermination policies based supposedly on sociobiology (p. 80). It is then no surprise that he is outraged by the publication of *Sociobiology: The New Synthesis* by Edward Wilson. For all its proposed objectivity, neutrality, and pure science, Wilson's book represents but another version of Nazi sociobiology (pp. 106–8).

We can give only samples of a very long list of sinners named by Chorover. He does not call them sinners, yet the entire book abounds with moral indignation. Perhaps the best term for Chorover's culprits is "sinful power brokers," since it includes theological language of sinfulness. Chorover finds that in Greek antiquity that both Plato and Aristotle were sinners, for they engaged in the power play. Plato's Myth of the Metals justified the current stratification of Greek society with all its injustices. Aristotle used his philosophy to justify slavery. Augustine was a sinner because he used the doctrine of original sin to keep the masses dependent upon the church.

In the third chapter Chorover discusses the abuse of power in intelligence testing of children and adults. Intelligence tests have been used to justify the thesis that people in power are rightfully there. The poor are poor and the powerless are weak and blacks are inferior because intelligence tests prove it. This chapter indicts such sinners as the educational psychologist Arthur Jensen, Sir Francis Galton, famous for his studies of genius, Stanford professors Lewis M. Terman, Ellwood P. Cubberly, and C. B. Davenport (and many more!).

In the fourth chapter the spotlight turns on American immigration policies to show they were not based on real scientific data about peoples and races. Rather, the policies were made by groups in America who favored one group of immigrants over another and used common prejudices, unsifted opinion, and plain wrong data to justify their policies in the name of science. The worst sinners of the group were scientists who supplied the politicians with worthless information bearing the name of valid research. Today we know that what they based their decisions upon is, according to real standards of scientific research, pure garbage. Chorover says this is not innocent error, for it was inspired by those who were in power and determined to stay there.

In the fifth chapter the sinners are sociobiologists. These are scientists who want to make the world safe for their kind by eliminating the unfit and valueless people who do nothing but consume the food supply. He spends much time showing that long before Hitler there were in Germany sociobiological theories whose eventual fruit was the gas chamber. Again Chorover points out that all this research and all exterminations of the mentally ill in Germany were carried on at the highest levels of academia by the most prominent members of the medical community.

His sixth chapter, on drug abuse, claims that drug control in this country is accomplished mainly by politicians whose policies are dictated by their (sinful) will to stay in power. Drug control is not based on truly scientific knowledge of the nature of drugs (the area of Chorover's doctoral research) nor on the proper psychological-sociological study of the people who use drugs.

The seventh chapter contains a brief history of psychosurgery and its modern application in psychiatric practice. His thesis in this chapter is that many who perform this kind of surgery are sinfully irresponsible. He examines the case of a patient labeled Thomas R. who was operated on to relieve his neurotic symptoms but who instead was psychologically destroyed.

The last chapter is devoted to penitentiaries and treatment of criminals. One can predict his diagnosis, namely, that the treatment of criminals is finally determined by politicians. Therefore the policies are sinfully dictated by political expediency rather than by a careful and trustworthy body of information about criminals.

We have given this much space to Chorover's book for a number of reasons. First, it shows that sin and sinfulness are not the special territories of the poor or the minorities or the illiterate, but sin invades the highest ranges of scientific pursuit. An examination of the book also shows how Chorover contradicts himself by voting with Pelagius, then filling a book with illustrations that prove the Augustinian point of view. One cannot explain sin in such high echelons of science from a Pelagian point of view, but it is consistent with the Augustinian view. It is also remarkable that Chorover's thesis is identical to that of C. S. Lewis in his book, *That Hideous Strength*.[29] In that book Lewis writes of a group of scientific sociologists who in the name of doing good for England wishes to take over all of England and impose its policies on the masses. The scoundrels of Belbury Place in Lewis's novel are the same scoundrels of Chorover's book.

Chorover does not fully examine human evil, for he centers on one major theme of it. Nor does he explain the psychological pathology that causes people to play the power control game. From Chorover's perspective the power play is evil; those who play it are evil; and the results on society are evil.[21]

XII

Albert Camus (1913–1960) lived a short forty-three years, but he took a long, penetrating, and severe look at the human condition. His first lesson in human depravity was his observations of Arab slums in Algeria where he was born, raised, and educated. His second lesson was his academic work in which he earned a master's degree in philosophy. His third lesson was his experience of World War II.

Asking Camus, "If Adam didn't, who did?" yields two answers. Camus was not a Christian; in fact he consciously rejected Christianity. But he was exposed to the Christian tradition. He could not major in philosophy in a French university without learning something of the history of Christian theology. His master's thesis dealt with the relationship of the philosophy of Plotinus to the thought of Augustine, and in reading Augustine he learned his theology of sin.

One of Camus's novels is entitled *The Fall*—certainly a Christian title. It is the story of a lawyer who hears the body of a young girl plunge into the Seine and does nothing to rescue her. Here is complete indifference of one human being toward another. In the preface Camus cites Mikhail Lermontov (1814–1841), a Russian romantic poet, saying in effect that The Fall of the lawyer from Paris was not one man's personal failure. Rather, *"it is the aggregate of the vices of our whole generation in their fullest expression* (p. viii)." This brutal indifference of human beings to one another was one of the sorest points in Camus's psyche. If he could not trace all the world's woes to it, certainly he suggested in *The Fall* that indifference plays an enormous role in human suffering.

However, his most detailed answer to the question of who sinned is in his novel *The Plague*.[23] Again Camus used a Christian title, for in his notebook on *The Plague* he referred to the biblical plagues of the book of Exodus as well as the plagues of Europe.

In briefest scope *The Plague* is the story of a North African town, Oran, being assulted by bubonic plague; the course of the plague as its intensity increased; the responses of various citizens of Oran; and finally the plague's subsidence and disappearance. Camus speaks his own mind through the town physician, Bernard Rieux.[24]

From the literary and psychological standpoints the genius of the book is its study of the various kinds of human transformation that take place under the conditions of the plague. The parallels with some of Dostoyevsky's characters is striking. Some very ordinary people attain heroism, and some solid citizens turn out to be, in the metaphor of the drama, rats. One important transformation is that of the Jesuit, Father Paneloux, who preaches two sermons. The first one is the typical moralistic, almost inhuman, sermon telling the citizens they suffer the plague because of their sins and therefore ought to repent. But due to suffering of the people and his compassionate work with the dying, Paneloux's second sermon is one of genuine spiritual compassion.

How is *The Plague* a secular version of the Christian doctrine of sin? First, its very title—*The Plague*—suggests that human existence itself is the plague. Although some would limit the book to a commentary on the Nazi invasion and takeover of much of France, or even World War II itself, Camus paints with a larger brush. Life is filled with sufferings, injustices, absurdities, and cruelties. Camus felt deepest about the suffering and death of little children and said through the mouth of Bernard Rieux, ". . . until my dying day I shall refuse to love a scheme of things in which little children are put to torture" (pp. 196–97).

Life is also plagued by absurdity and meaninglessness. Camus wrote a book about the Greek myth of Sisyphus.[25] Sisyphus is condemned eternally to roll a stone to the top of a hill only to have it roll down again. Life is plagued with absurdity, and death is the final absurdity of all.

Life is also plagued because none of the traditional stays of the human spirit remain in our century. There is no Eternal Good or Everlasting Father to aid plagued human existence. Whatever God there is sits in heaven in stony silence and in complete inaction. The "eternal verities" of the philosophers have been undermined by modern philosophical thought. The only power humanity has to deal with its problems and plagues must be found within itself.

When the plague has finally left Oran the citizens engage in a momentous celebration with fireworks. As Rieux sits by himself and meditates, he sums up his philosophy. When human existence is plagued one must do what one can as small as it may be. He as a physician did his best according to his calling. In the long run plagues produce more of the hero types than the rat types. But then comes the closing paragraph of the book—a paragraph Augustine or Luther or Calvin or Pascal could have written:

> And, indeed, as he listened to the cries of joy rising from the town, Rieux remembered that such joy is always imperiled. He knew what those jubilant crowds did not know but could have learned from books: that the plague bacillus never dies or disappears for good; that it can lie dormant for many years and years in furniture and linen-chests; that it bides its time in bedrooms, cellars, trunks, and bookshelves; and that perhaps the day would come when, for the bane and the enlightening of men, it would rouse up its rats again and send them forth to die in a happy city. (p. 278).

Not only is human existence plagued, but it is incurably plagued. This is indeed a secular version of human existence, coinciding well with the Christian doctrine of sin.

XIII

Although T. S. Eliot (1888–1965) was an affirmed Christian believer (as of the year 1927 when he was baptized into the Anglican Communion) his drama, *The Family Reunion*[26], deserves special attention at this point. It tries to convey the Christian doctrine of sin through the medium of drama and with the absolute minimum of theological language to a generation of English aristocracy who had lost complete sight of it. Beneath the various metaphors Eliot uses to express his views lies a strong Christian conception of sin. Some of Eliot's poems and dramas are very difficult for nonreligious people to understand, because they do not recognize the disguised Christian motifs. For example, one reviewer interpreted

The Family Reunion as a study of the generation gap in English high society. Certainly that element is present, but it is a mere backdrop. Others view *The Family Reunion* as a study of English types. That also is but a secondary motif.

Eliot had a profound respect for the Christian doctrine of depravity and did not think any person could be a great artist without a profound sense of the eternal struggle of good and evil in the human breast and in human society. *The Family Reunion* is a serious study of the doctrine of sin cast in the form of a drama to reach the modern age that has drifted so far from traditional Christian doctrines moorings.

The drama centers in Harry (formally, Lord Monchensey, the new lord of the family estate of Wishwood). In traditional Christian language Harry suffers from an acute case of conviction of sin brought about in the drama by his wife disappearing over the railing of an ocean vessel.

As a good dramatist Eliot sets out the doctrine of sin in a number of metaphors. Sin is described as an old house with leaky plumbing. The result is a stench in the house so permeating that no (human) plumber can get it out. Sin is presented as something deeper than cancer. It is deeper than the feelings of a guilty conscience, for humans are experts in shaping their consciences to suit their moods. Sin is likened to sobbing in a chimney and evil in a dark closet. It is also likened to upsetting noises like bumps in the cellar or the unexpected rattling of windows. It is called a private puzzle. And it is openly identified as a desperate case of filthiness.

In many different turns of words and metaphors Eliot tells us how uncomfortable the concept of sin makes modern people. They do now want doors or windows opened. They don't want to hear sounds for which there is no accounting. They want the river of their lives to flow with no ripples.

Eliot describes these modern sophisticates as totally incapable of understanding Harry. Having no concept of depravity or sin or the experience of the conviction of sin they have no way of comprehending Harry's dilemma. They bring in the family doctor to see if he can talk some sense into Harry, but it is the doctor who finds himself confounded. In a burst of supposed illumination they think Harry wants to become a missionary—about the most trite and superficial of diagnoses. Eliot is correct; the bulk of intellectuals and sophisticates of the twentieth century have no understanding of the Christian doctrine of sin.

Eliot affirms that the resolution of Harry's problem is the Christian gospel. Eliot does not use the words God or Christ or the gospel. But he does use metaphors that can refer only to the gospel, such as untying the knot, straightening up the crossed bones, making the crooked straight, completing the charm, and the following the bright angels.

XIV

From our very brief review of alternative, secular accountings of human misery some conclusions may be drawn.

1. Ernst Cassirer was right in observing that when the Christian doctrine of Original Sin was denied at the time of the Enlightenment, the traditional litany of human miseries still had to be accounted for on other grounds. The evils theologians attributed to Original Sin remained in society, and if the Christian answer was inadequate a secular answer needed to be found.

2. It is remarkable how many of these secular accounts of Original Sin are unwittingly based on Christian premises. In many instances the proffered theory is part of the Christian interpretation.

3. Most important, the review shows that the Christian doctrine of Original Sin (or of sin) is not an esoteric, in-house, intramural Christian topic. It is not a theme known only to gnostic Christian initiates. It is a problem at the center of both personal and social life. It concerns the endless series of crimes police forces must deal with. It is about personal tragedies leading to divorce courts and counselors' studies. It is about brutality, rape, torture, and war. It concerns the perpetual problems educators encounter in the classroom. It is not only about the grubby pickpocket, but criminal decisions in the offices of large corporations. It is about

the Mafia, the numbers racket, and the enormous drug traffic. It concerns the cruel sexual abuse of children and the problems of violence and degradation in penitentiaries. It is about small lies and the betrayal of one's country.

The Christian with an open mind can learn something from each of these secular versions of human sin and evil. The following chapters will show that the Christian doctrine of sin, while not denying that Christians can learn from other sources, is the most comprehensive and satisfying explanation of personal and social ills.

3. The Case Against the Human Race

No world religion has such an extensive doctrine of sin as Christianity. It is one of the leading themes in both the Old and New Testaments. G. C. Berkouwer, who has written extensively on the theology of sin, states that one point in Holy Scripture can never be challenged or qualified: God is never to be imagined as either the author or the cause of sin. This he calls the biblical a priori.[1] Furthermore, among world religions no such concept of the holiness of God exists as is in Old Testament materials. The Lord is a God who dwells in radiant glory, in absolute holiness, purity, and justice. Sinners who might stumble into this presence would instantly die.

But this concept of the impeccable holiness of God needs to be seen from another perspective, the Christological position. We do not know how to imagine, comprehend, measure, or conceptualize the divine reaction to sin until we know the divine remedy to sin, namely, that the Son of God had to go the way of the cross to solve the problem posed by our sin. After indicting the whole world as sinful before God, Paul introduces the remedy as supplied by "an expiation by his blood" (Rom. 3:25). In the summary of the Christian gospel in 1 Cor. 15:1–8 Paul says that Christ was crucified for our sins. In each of these cases the measure of sin must be read backwards from the cross. Critical in a special sense is Rom. 5:12–21. The great tragedy introduced by the defection of Adam can only be properly framed, grasped, or understood from the great victory of grace in Jesus Christ. Anselm (1033–1109) is famous for his question, "Who has truly pondered the weight of sin?" The answer is, "The one who has truly pondered the weight of the cross."

This might be one of the reasons why Gen. 3 stands without comment in the rest of the Old Testament. It introduces a problem that cannot really be clarified until the Son of God takes our flesh, assumes our burden, and bears it away on the cross as the one, true Lamb of God (cf. John 1:29).

Furthermore, historical, theological reflection connecting the cross and the incarnation is further commentary—although not always understood that way—that the doctrine of sin can only be understood reflexively from the cross. We have in mind Athanasius's (296–373) *The Incarnation of the Word of God*, Anselm's *Cur Deus Homo?* and the theological reflections of Martin Luther (1483–1546) and John Calvin (1509–1564).

In the following pages we will investigate the divine indictment of humanity as sinful. We will not assume that the doctrine or concept of sin is simple to define, or that it can be done apart from reference to other doctrines. We take the measure of sin from the cross. If all have sinned and come short of the glory of God, we will assume that we cannot understand that "coming short" apart from the cross.

Before we look at texts which speak of human sin and the case Scripture makes against the human race, we must note two interlocked criteria such a case must include. First, the scope of the indictment must be nothing short of the whole world, of every creature, of every human who has lived, is living, or will yet live. Anything short of that would reduce the Christian gospel to a limited, parochial scope. The second criterion is inevitability. The case is lost if some or a few or even one squeak through unscathed by sin (the blessed Redeemer being the sole exception and that for the very reason of the gospel and not on the basis of some Christian hagiography or unbridled veneration of the Founder).

Many texts in Scripture simply announce directly or by implication the universal sinfulness of the race and offer no underlying explanation.[2]

Job 14:1–22 laments the frailty of the human person. The human person is unclean, and therefore cannot bring forth clean persons—not one! (v. 4). Jer. 17 also reflects on the nature of human existence. Right in the midst of this meditation are the words, "The heart is deceitful above all things, and desperately corrupt;

who can understand it?" (v. 9). The implied answer is that the heart is too corrupt to be understood. In Rom. 3:23 Paul states categorically that all have sinned and come short of the glory of God. One interpretation is that the glory of God in the text is a shaft of light of the shekinah glory that shone on Adam. When Adam sinned it disappeared. That no person today bears that shaft of glory is witness to universal sinfulness. In Gal. 3:22 Paul says that God confines the universe (*ta panta*) to sin in order to introduce the gospel of salvation. Similarly, in Rom. 11:32 he says that God consigns all to disobedience.

Many other such texts appear on the pages of Holy Scripture. G. C. Berkouwer asserts that such verses reflect the divine verdict upon the race. He is reluctant to look for an underlying theory binding all persons together in one family of sinners. Rather he emphasizes that this is God's verdict; it is a true verdict, and we should spiritually come to terms with it.

In some contrast to Berkouwer, we state again that all these texts of both Old and New Testaments must be seen Christologically. We cannot measure how sinful or how unclean or how disobedient the sinner is, or how scarlet our sins are, apart from the divine remedy in the cross. From the standpoint of the gospel these verses do not rest alone with a completely transparent meaning or significance of their own.

In other words, there is no abstract measurement of the seriousness and nature of sin. Sin may be defined as transgressing the law, but that does not measure its seriousness. Only in the remedy of the cross do we gain some sense of the measure of sin. In the cross we see what was needed to cure it.

II

Some have said that Jesus never spoke of Adam as the author of all human sin, not did he refer to the Fall or to Original Sin. If this implies that Jesus took sin lightly, then the strong and pervasive theology of sin found in the Gospels has been overlooked. To discover how Scriptures indict the entire world as sinful, we must ask if any of the sayings of Christ suggest his views on the matter. Two texts especially emerge.

The first text deals with the human heart (Matt. 5:16–20, Mark 7:20–23). Hans Walter Wolff's extensive discussion of the heart in the Old Testament is helpful here.[3] After discussing the heart as a physical organ Wolff discusses heart as a psychological term. Used in a psychological sense the heart is a very rich concept, including feelings, wishes, and rational thought. No simple definition can do it justice.

This complex nature of the heart enables us to understand all those references in the Old Testament locating sin in the human heart. As S. J. de Vries points out, one of the major Old Testament theories of the origin of sin is the corrupt heart.[4] The human heart can be impure, rebellious, and hard.

Our Lord's statement about the heart should be understood in this context of the Old Testament view of the heart. Matthew lists evil thoughts, sexual immorality, theft, murder, adultery, false testimony, and slander as the sins that emerge from the wicked heart. Mark's list is longer, adding such sins as greed, malice, deceit, lewdness, envy, arrogance, and folly.

If the heart is a synonym for the psyche in its complexity, and if sin bubbles out of that center, then the human person is truly a sinner. The language of Jesus is strong, emphatic, and precise. The heart as the mission-control center of the person is the source of sin, and therefore we are sinners. Our Lord simply takes over the Old Testament understanding of the wicked heart without speculating how the heart became wicked.

In Matt. 7:11 and Luke 11:13 (cf. John 8:46) Jesus speaks out directly and inclusively, telling his listeners that they are evil. He uses the participle, "you being evil." No doubt this statement also is rooted in the Old Testament. It is generally true in the Old Testament that when God and humanity are morally compared and contrasted, God is holy and/or good, and humanity is evil. Evil in this sense means a spiritually defined evil, such as wrong attitudes towards God, hardness of heart, or making wicked choices. As such, Jesus' assertion that his listeners are evil is in harmony with

Paul's later indictment of the whole world. Jesus did not take sin lightly. He accepted the Old Testament teaching that the heart is desperately wicked, and that humanity when contrasted with God (in moral categories) will always appear wicked.

There is no neat statement in the Gospels that all have sinned and come short of the glory of God as Paul wrote in Rom. 3:23. But in the statements that our Lord came to die for the whole world and that the gospel is to be preached in the whole world are founded in the necessary assumption that the whole world is sinful, lost, and in need of redemption.

III

Rom. 1:18–3:20 is one text of Scripture whose purpose is to prove that the entire race is sinful. We will not interpret the text here but attempt to lay bare the logic of the case. We want to expose the method by which Paul conclusively indicts humanity.

The range of the indictment is the entire human race. This is expressed by the phrases "every mouth" (3:19), "the whole world" (3:19), and "no human being" (3:20). The expression "Jews and Gentiles" (3:9) as well as "all men" (3:9) express the same universal indictment.

Indictment I: Humanity proves itself sinful by persistently misreading the witness of creation to a powerful, spiritual Deity (1:17–32). The unexpressed thesis is that a person with a pure mind, untouched by sin, would look at creation and immediately and spiritually intuit the Creator without distortion. As sinners, none of us has any idea of the nature of that experience, just as congenitally blind people have no idea of color.

From the sinner's failure to intuit the true Creator two other sinful consequences follow. In place of the worship of the true Creator, idolatry of every imaginable type emerges. Ethically the life of the sinner is characterized by immorality. Certainly Paul, "the Roman Traveler," saw in all his journeys that the religion of his times was characterized by idolatry and immorality.

Indictment II: Humanity proves itself sinful by violating every moral criterion by which it assesses itself (2:1–11). Sinners cannot save themselves from moral inconsistency. Paul contrasts human moral inconsistency with the perfect moral consistency of God's judgments.

Indictment III: Humanity proves itself sinful by falling short of every given standard of moral excellence (2:12–29). Paul uses the law as such a standard, both in the sense of a written code possessed by the nation of Israel, and the unwritten code of the human heart found in the Gentile world. Those who live under the written code come short of it (but this involves Paul in a complex analysis of the Jews and the law, 2:17–29). The Gentiles, not having the law written down in specific sentences but having instead a series of moral impressions, do not always know what is right or wrong. Hence Paul says they must always carry on an internal apologetic about the propriety of their actions (2:15).

Indictment IV: Humanity proves itself sinful by turning every privileged role or blessing in the kingdom of God into judgment, not spiritual prosperity (3:1–8). Having the law not only gave the Jewish people the divine specifics, it gave them also a divine privilege. However, the privilege turned into a further judgment because sinners invariably turn privileges into occasions for abuse. Paul does not argue that the Jews are sinners because they abused privileges, but rather being sinners it logically follows that they will abuse privileges.

Indictment V: Humanity proves itself sinful because this is the verdict of the inspired Scriptures of the nation of Israel (3:9–18). Here Paul puts together in rabbinic fashion a chain of Old Testament phrases. He apparently thinks that Jewish readers of the letter might assume he is simply expressing his own views. By adding a chain of biblical texts from the Old Testament Paul affirms that all he says can be verified by the divinely inspired Jewish Scriptures.

From the standpoint of logic the language is more than significant. In formal logic, the absence of examples of a proposed entity is called a null or empty class (for instance, the class of six-legged elephants is an empty or null class). If all entities are included in a class it is a full class (all people are mortal is a full class). Paul indicates by the use of *no, not one, no one, none*, and *not even one* that the class of people who so please God that they need no salvation is a null or empty class. By his use of *all* and *together* he indicates that the class of the unrighteous needing salvation is a full class.

Paul wishes to make one other point, namely, the degree of human depravity. This he does by taking different parts of the human body and speaking metaphorically of their powers of evil or corruption. His point is well made, for it shows that the entire psyche has come under the influence of sin. Sinners are not only barren of righteousness and possessed of guilt, but corrupt in nature. The indictment is complete.

The scope of Paul's indictment is the whole of humanity. The indictment is set out in five theses. And the way is now prepared for Paul to introduce the saving work of Christ. Perhaps the greatest transition in Holy Scripture is the one from Rom. 3:20 to 3:21. Up to Rom. 3:20 Paul labored hard to establish the indictment of the race as both sinful and guilty. Then in Rom. 3:20 he inserts with no connectives at all the great redeeming work of Christ. This in turn causes us to reflect on the thesis that the entire indictment is not in focus until Christ and his redemptive work is introduced. It is then redemption in Christ that leads us to look backwards over the history of the indictment to know specifically what the indictment amounts to.

IV

Ephesians is also a key book in the indictment of the world as full of sinners. The church of Ephesus comprised both Jewish and Gentile Christians. If Ephesians was a general letter addressed to many churches (for "in Ephesus" of Eph. 1:1 is lacking in the better manuscripts), the situation would have been similar. Ephesians had to speak for the most part to the Christians of a Gentile origin, and so its method contrasts with that employed in Romans. Again our concern is not the detailed exegesis of the text but an examination of the nature of the cause that Paul makes in his indictment.

The first text is Eph. 2:1–3. Like Rom. 1:17–3:20 the indictment is universal. In Eph. 2:3 Paul uses the expression *hoi polloi*—the remainder, everybody else, or as the RSV says, "the rest of mankind." This means that the indictment is not limited to the readership of the letter, or the territory of Asia Minor, but it includes the whole world.

This is a highly concentrated text with one phrase qualifying another, making a simple explanation of Paul's argument difficult. Paul indicts the Ephesians with spiritual death. The Greek word for dead (in this text) is *nekros*. The word is used often in the New Testament (more than sixty times) and refers not only to physical death but also to metaphorical and figurative death (for instance, dead works, the dead Prodigal Son, the dead church). In Eph. 2:1 *nekros* means spiritually lifeless, spiritually inert, or totally unresponsive to the promptings of God. 1 Tim. 5:6 illustrates this meaning well. The widow who is self-indulgent "is [spiritually] dead even while she yet lives [physiologically, psychologically, socially]."

Paul next introduces the cause of the state of death. Spiritual death among the Ephesians is caused by walking in transgressions (literally, false steps) and sins. Paul uses the Greek verb *peripateō* in his own special sense. To walk in transgressions and sins (against God and God's holiness) means daily to conduct one's life in such a pattern. The indictment does not mean that here and there these people have sinned. Rather, the entire course of their lives is involved in transgressions and sins. The indictment is then that these people are sinners because their daily conduct involves them in sinning.

Paul moves from the affirmation of spiritual death, to the charge of walking in transgressions and sins, to a third charge: being *sons of disobedience*. In Hebrew thought a person specifically characterized by something was called a child of that characteristic. So Paul's charge means that the lives of these people were characterized by disobedience to God. Hence walking in transgressions and sins is synonymous with being a child of disobedience.

Paul then increases the indictment by showing another ingredient in this walk of death and disobedience. The sinners walk a course of life planned and "grooved" by Satan. He uses the word *aion* that has many meanings in the Greek language and the New Testament. It could mean two things in Eph. 2:2. Since *aion* in many instances is a synonym for world, some translations read "the course of this world," i.e., the typical life of the sinners, and the ungodly. It can also mean a ruler, hence a person. In this sense Paul is identifying Satan with two expressions: (1) the ruler of this world, and (2) the prince of the power of the air (a Jewish expression to denote the area of the rulership of Satan). But the sense of the passage is the same no matter how we translate *aion*. Sinners walking in transgressions, sins, and disobedience are conducting their lives under a satanic influence.

It is very important to note specifically what Paul says about Satan. He does not identify Satan with anything abnormal, unusual, manifestly demonic, or dramatic. Instead, he identifies the role of Satan with the daily rut, the daily grind, the so-called 9-to-5 day, the common routine. Our daily chatter, our daydreaming, our way of relating to people, the decisions of value, and the decisions of morality are the matters cluttering up every day's activity. In this connection Paul introduces a third characterization of Satan—the spirit who energizes children of disobedience.

This is a profound piece of biblical anthropology. 1 John 4:1 indicates that besides the inward operation of the human psyche *a spirit* is also at work. Therefore Christians are to test spirits. This is of course something a behaviorist would utterly and emphatically deny. But, as we noticed with Ernest Becker, the human psyche responds to all sorts of images, symbols, and psychic pictures. That is a spirit at work! And Sigmund Freud's theory of the unconscious using the symbolism of id, superego, and ego, his almost unlimited number of sexual images (e.g., all box-shaped things in the dream world are disguised images of the vagina), and his elaborate theory of dream interpretation all suggest a spirit at work (even though Freud pictured himself as a hard, tough, empirical scientist). C. Gustav Jung's psychiatric theory moves even further into the world of symbols. In addition to the unconscious he postulates the collective unconscious and universal archetypes. Here too a spirit is at work. A pedestrian analysis of human behavior never gets to the heart of the matter.

Next Paul wants to show that sinners are not only *sons of disobedience* but also *by nature children of wrath*. So the indictment of Eph. 2:1–3 continues.

Again Paul uses a Greek verb (*anastrephō*—as *peripateō*) to indicate the whole of life, the daily routine of life, or the conduct of life according to certain principles. Sinners as a matter of daily routine conduct their lives according to the passions of the flesh, which means they follow the desires of the body and the mind. Note that in addition to *flesh* as the fulcrum for sin he adds the mind (*dianoia*). We know that committing crimes and sinning in general are not the results of being pushed and pulled by lowly passions, but also involve much thinking, much cerebration. Paul indicts the mind as well as the flesh.

We now come to a *crux interpretum*, a text that is very difficult to interpret. Texts of this type result in strongly competing interpretations, since they often stand at the crossroads of an argument. What does the phrase *by nature children of wrath* mean? More particularly, what does *by nature* (*physis*) mean?

A long hermeneutical tradition refers the text to the Fall of Adam, giving it the meaning that we are all fallen *by nature*. As creatures with a fallen nature the only possible divine verdict is wrath. As Walter Bauer puts it in his lexicon: "We were, in our natural condition (as descendants of Adam) children of wrath."[5]

More recent opinion understands *by nature* to mean the long history of the sinner as a sinner. The sinful person is so habitually a sinner that it has become, in the American idiom, second nature. Someone so habituated to sinning is therefore only worthy of the wrath of God and is called a child of wrath.

A third opinion is that Paul is informing the Jewish readers that they too are sinners like the Gentiles and are not exempt from the wrath of God as some of their scholars have taught. *By nature* then means that Jews are as genuinely sinful as Gentiles.

In the interpretation of this text it is difficult to determine which versions are the result of a growing rejection of the Augustinian view of sin and which are based on more informed knowledge of the Greek language. Either way Paul's indictment stands. Jews and Gentiles are by nature children of wrath, whether *by nature* means an inherited sinful nature or whether it means a sinner in virtue of a long career of habitual sinning.

In Ephesians 2:12 Paul introduces an indictment of another order. Indictments of sinnerhood usually rotate around such concepts as law or the holiness of God. That there might be another method comes as a complete surprise to us in Ephesians. When Paul took his stance in the salvation-history concept a different kind of indictment surfaced. Paul measures the sinfulness of the Gentiles as it contrasts with the salvation-history phenomenon of Israel. Consider the difference between the Gentile moral and spiritual life, and Israel, and the sinfulness of the Gentile emerges in a new light and in a new perspective. We could also call it an alternative to the Christological method of proving that all the world has sinned and come short of the glory of God revealed in the face of Jesus Christ. As we have said, we can only truly ponder the weight of sin in the light of the person and work of Jesus Christ.

Paul says that judged from this salvation-history perspective the Gentiles are (1) without Christ, (2) excluded from the [divine] commonwealth of Israel, (3) estranged from the covenants of promise, (4) having no hope, and (5) atheists in the world. The latter phrase can be taken in two ways. It may mean that they are atheists in that they do not worship the true and living God. But it more likely means that Gentiles are bereft of the providential care of God enjoyed by those within the flow of salvation-history.

A parallel kind of indictment is found in Eph. 2:19. Measured against salvation-history (in the sense Paul presents it in Ephesians and not necessarily some sophisticated theological interpretation of the phrase), Gentile sinfulness is measured by two criteria: (1) Gentiles are foreigners in the sense that they have no lawful status in God's on-going salvation-history; and (2) they are sojourners in the sense that as visitors in a land they have no legal rights to the blessings of salvation-history.

A third and yet again different kind of indictment occurs in Eph. 4:17–23. Right in the midst of it is the phrase "you did not so learn Christ" (v. 20). In this case the purity of Christ measures the sinful impurity of the Gentiles and so indicts them as sinners. The Christological principle not only shows the sinful spiritual alienation of Gentiles but also their moral corruption. Paul again in a very compact manner piles sin upon sin: futility of mind, darkened understanding, hardness of heart, spiritual and moral callousness, licentiousness, greedy practices, every kind of un-cleanness, deceitful lusts. Any newspaper of a large metropolitan area will every day verify every sin on Paul's list.

Two things may be said of Paul's indictment of the race as sin-ful as set out in Ephesians. First, in the phrase of Sir William Ram-say, the founder of New Testament archeology, Paul was a World Traveler. He knew the Roman Empire via its towns and cities from Jerusalem to Rome. Clearly, he used the Empire as a paradigm of the sinful character of the whole world. Paul read from the pages of life when he described sinful humanity, and therefore his in-dictment bears a powerful, empirical ring. It is not scholarly, iso-lated speculation.

The second observation is that Paul does not speak of sin as if it were an obviously autonomous category. Rather he reveals the baseline for his indictment. Broadly speaking it is salvation-histo-ry, and in narrower terms it is Christology. In reply to Anselm who asked who has truly pondered the weight of sin, the answer is, those who truly understand salvation-history and Jesus Christ.

V

Scholars generally agree that Paul wrote 1 Corinthians before he wrote Romans. Thus his first reference to Adam appears in 1 Cor. 15:20–50 while Rom. 5:12–21 represents later reflections. In 1 Corinthians Paul discusses the resurrection, contrasting the frail, earthy, weak Adam with the powerful, glorious Man from Heaven. Nowhere in the text does he introduce sin. Paul says that by Adam came death (v. 22), but he does not attribute it to sin. The entire chapter attributes death to the frailty of the earthly human. If the notion of sin is in the chapter, it certainly stands deep in the shadows.

However, matters are very different in Rom. 5:12–21. This text has been called the most difficult passage to interpret in the entire New Testament, and none who explore it can doubt this assertion.[6]

The basic character of the text is that Paul is not primarily dealing with the indictment of humanity as sinful. He is instead describing the glorious redemption in Christ (the formal indictment appears in Rom. 1:17–3:20). Augustine was the one who interpreted the passage as pertaining to the indictment of humanity as sinful. The result is that functionally speaking the indictment of Rom. 1:17–3:20 is replaced by Rom. 5:12–21. The problem began with a mistake in translation. Augustine's Latin text of Rom. 5:12 read *in quo*, which means "in whom." Hence to Augustine it meant "in Adam." The entire human race fell in the sin of Adam, and all are therefore born into the world as unregenerate lost sinners. The Greek text reads *eph'hō* which means "because of." As such it connects the fall of Adam with the sinful state of the race but does not specify the nature of the connection.

It is not difficult to discern why Rom. 5:12–21 has functionally displaced Rom. 1:17–3:20 as the basic indictment of the human race. It makes such a neat, simple parallel between Adam and Christ, a parallel that has proven irresistible to theologians.

The second problem with the text is that it speaks in generalities describing two great families, the Adam-family and the Christ-family, but it does not specify how the individual is as a matter of fact connected with either of the families. We know that the connection with the Christ-family is by faith in Jesus Christ, for Paul devoted the entire fourth chapter of Romans to explain how Abraham is the father of all who believe and are so justified. But Rom. 5:12–21 says nothing about faith or personal confession of Christ as the connecting link between the believer and Christ.

Neither does it explain how sinners are connected to Adam and hence are in fact sinners. The theological connectors linking the families of Adam and Christ are not in the text; they can only be read into it.

The entire New Testament clearly testifies that believers are spiritually united to Christ by faith and by the Holy Spirit. But how is the sinner related to Adam? If too much emphasis is put on biological succession from Adam, sin takes on the shape of a biological substance not unlike a defective gene. Even worse, Augustine believed sin was passed on by sexual intercourse. Sin is not a biological substance nor a defective gene. Sin belongs to the categories of the moral and spiritual.

How vexing this problem can be is illustrated from a page of the history of American theology. A very independent English scholar, John Taylor (1694–1761), wrote a book (*Scripture Doctrine of Original Sin*, 1740) in which he denied the traditional Augustinian doctrine. The book was carried by sailing vessel to America. When it arrived in America it stirred up a great debate reviewed for us by H. Shelton Smith's *Changing Concepts of Original Sin*.[7]

The crux of the problem is *alien guilt*. Personal sin engenders personal guilt. How then can the sin of Adam (personal guilt to him) by imputed to countless unborn generations who were not alive at the time but are yet guilty (*alien guilt*)? Even the great effort of Jonathan Edwards to settle the issue failed.[8]

No one was able to untie the knot of alien guilt, so the debate subsided. Smith notes in his last chapter that the debate has been revived in the twentieth century but with radically different reformulations.[9]

Before we attempt to come to our own terms with the text, some review of the options is necessary.

VI

The issue in the debate over Rom. 5:12–21 is by what means the sin of Adam is connected with the sinfulness of the rest of humanity. How can an act at the headwaters of the human race affect every human being born since then? What point was Paul affirming in the text? The following is an all-too-brief summary of some of the more significant theories attempting to show the nature of the connection between Adam and the race.

1. Surveys of patristic literature from the second century to Augustine reveal that most theologians assumed a general connection between Adam and the race, but none reflected profoundly upon it. Irenaeus (130–200) taught a theology of recapitulation. While Adam and Eve failed in their temptation, Christ and Mary repeated the temptation under more adverse circumstances and succeeded in remaining obedient. Hence they procured salvation. Origen (185–254) taught a fall of souls in their preexistence (for he was much influenced by Plato). Tertullian (160–225) most nearly approached an articulate doctrine of Original Sin with his idea that sin is passed on as part of one's total inheritance from one's parents (traducianism). In general, the most widely held opinion was the weakened race theory. Adam's sin weakened him and all his descendants so that they inevitably sin.

2. In the organic race theory Adam is interpreted as both a person and a race. Just as Levi was in the reproductive organs of Abraham (*osphus*) when Abraham met Melchizedek (Heb. 7:10), so the entire human race was seminally in Adam. Every human being derived from Adam was in the Garden in the person of Adam, so all are cosinners with Adam.

3. The platonic-ideal theory of W. G. T. Shedd, one of America's great theologians of the nineteenth century, and Jonathan Edwards, teaches that all human beings are struck from Adam just as coins are struck in a mint from the master die. In the platonic sense of forms or archetypes the entire race is thus present in Adam. If there was a flaw in the archetype (Adam) then every copy (ektype) struck from the archetype will carry the same flaw. Thus as God reproduces the race after the divine pattern of Adam, the flaw of original sin must be reproduced in each member of the human race.

4. Johannes Cocceius (1603–1669) was a Dutch theologian who developed the notion of federal theology. In this theology the

human race is related to God on a convenantal basis. This was interpreted as both a personal covenant and a broader social covenant. Hence sinners are related to Adam covenantally, and believers are related to Christ covenantally. This view became popular in Geneva and François Turrentini (1617–1737) of Geneva wrote a theological textbook based on federal theology. The great Presbyterian theologian of the nineteenth century in America, Charles Hodge (1797–1878), used Turrentini's textbook in his teaching at Princeton Theological Seminary and incorporated it into his own *Systematic Theology* (3 vols.). Through the writings of Hodge, federal theology became widely adopted in American theology, especially among evangelicals and fundamentalists.

Federal theology teaches that Adam and Christ were each sovereignly appointed by God to be the head and therefore representative for each of their families. That to which the federal head binds himself is bound upon each member of the family. When Adam sinned he therefore legally and lawfully bound all descendants to the state of sin, depravity, and guilt. Like a representative government where all citizens are bound to the laws enacted by their legally elected representatives, the federal headship of Adam is a kind of representation. All citizens have already agreed to the governance of Adam.

5. Under the name Vigilius Haufniensis, Søren Kierkegaard published a book with the long title: *The Concept of Anxiety: A Simple Psychologically Orienting Deliberation on the Dogmatic Issue of Hereditary Sin.*[10] Although originally published in 1844, it has exerted an enormous influence on twentieth-century theology. Kierkegaard registered a protest in this book. He believed that both the traditional Lutheran and the federal doctrines of Adam and Original Sin put Adam outside the race so that he is not truly our father. The traditional interpretation pictures Adam in a sinless state or *status integritatis* in the Garden. When he disobeys he falls into depravity and Original Sin. But this picture is not true of any of us; we are born—in the familiar Latin expression—*in medias res*, in the midst of things. Older views of Adam placed Adam outside of history.

Adam must be put back into history. This is done by understanding Gen. 3 not as a myth nor as literal history but as an existential cross section of the primal act of sinning. This is not a superficial rerun of the old maxim that we are each our own Adam, but a profound existential analysis as to why as a matter of fact and necessity we do sin. In simplest of terms, Kierkegaard argues that freedom to be and to choose arouses our anxiety. This anxiety leads us to make the leap into sin. We cannot trace the chain of causes that led us to sin, since that would be a natural psychological explanation. Rather Kierkegaard sets up the conditions under which we do make the qualitative leap into sin. This concept of sin positing itself is difficult to get a hold of. Basically it means a decision of the sovereign self. If in any manner we could explain the act of sinning by psychological or sociological studies and show how a person was caused to sin, the act would cease to be sin. Sin is only sin when a person freely postulates it as his or her action. It was not until the intensive studies of Kierkegaard in the twentieth century that this concept was understood and began to influence twentieth-century theology.

6. Karl Barth expressed many old ideas in new ways. It is never clear whether he is saying something old in a new, fresh way or introducing something very new. This is the predicament we face when we read Barth's special commentary on Rom. 5:11–21.[11]

Present comments are limited to the manner in which Barth sees the human race's connection with Adam. He believes that humanity was created as the weak, frail vessel of the first Adam described in 1 Cor. 15:20–50. Barth notes Rom. 5:6 where we are described as weak and ungodly. We are also sinners (5:8) and enemies (5:10). In other words, Adam was not created with a sinless nature and open ability to obey or disobey God. Adam means weakness, dust, and frailty. Barth does say that humanity is in the image of God, and sinful humanity possesses genuine humanity. But Adam is all and all are Adam. Barth therefore says each of us is Adam, but also that insofar as we reflect universal humanity we each are a race.

Thus Adam is a code name for several characters: the first human being to appear on the face of the earth; the whole human race as it is in Adam's image; and each person as a frail, weak, guilty sinner.[12]

7. Another effort to link humanity with Adam arises from H. Wheeler Robinson's book, *Corporate Personality in Ancient Israel*.[13] Robinson says that in Israel a group could be treated as if it were one individual. Likewise, one person could act as the whole group. A family, a town, a clan, a tribe, and a nation under certain conditions could be treated as if it were one person; in another context the king could incorporate all of Israel. Similar patterns exist in the New Testament where all believers are pictured as one entity (temple, body), and Christ in turn is a corporate name for all Christians.

Adam then becomes the supreme corporate personality in whom the whole human race is envisioned as one person. This may well be much closer to Old Testament ways of thinking than federal theology, but the Gordian knot (i.e., how Adam is related to all of humanity) remains uncut.

Paul does unite Adam and Christ by the use of the word *type* (Rom. 5:14). A type is some institution or person or practice in the Old Testament that anticipates its counterpart in the New Testament. Adam as the head of the old humanity is the type of Christ who is the head of the new humanity. As long as the comparison is understood in general terms no difficulty arises. The problem emerges anew when we attempt to explain how all people are of necessity sinners in view of the sin of the first human being—the problem of *alien guilt*.

However perplexing Rom. 5:12–21 may be, we must come to some terms with it.

1. The theme of the passage is that the triumph of the grace of God in Jesus Christ is greater than the tragedy of sin occasioned by Adam. If grace is so triumphant it raises a question: *why not sin more to increase grace?* The sixth chapter of Romans is given over to show that cannot be. In other words, the passage does not end with a summary statement of human sinfulness, but with a hypothetical question that an all-conquering grace suggests.

When this chapter serves as the main indictment of sinful humanity, then the central theme of the text is obscured.

2. The text does present us with the two great families of the human race: the fallen family of Adam and the redeemed family of Christ. By using the word city rather than family Augustine organized the whole history of Scripture (in his work, *The City of God*) into the City of God and the City of Man (or, the City of Sin).

3. The text repeats in its own way the material in Gen. 2–11. Creation is the beginning of history; the climax of creation is male and female in the image of God; the first human is the first sinner; and with the sin of the first human begins the miserable sinful history of humanity.

4. The text concerns realities of forces, powers, and energies. Sin is not seen so much as a formal breaking of a specified law but as a contagious disease that spreads through a population. It reminds us of the opening of Pandora's box where the evils of the world take their flight. Death also is not seen so much as the physiological termination of life but as a blight, a power, an irresistible, undeniable force. Death is said *to rule*—a strong verb occurring five times in the text. Also present are the very active verbs *to abound* and to *hyper-abound*. The whole mood, again, suggests powers and triumphs; forcing the exposition into forensic or static categories distorts the text. This distortion happens when the text is used as the formal indictment of humanity as sinful.

In Berkouwer's large book on sin (two volumes in the original Dutch) he never clearly formulates his theory of the connection between Adam and the rest of the sinful race. He does not slice away at the Gordian knot but simply assumes the connection as a datum of divine revelation. In this he is wise, for the text of Rom. 5:12–21 does not reveal the manner in which generic Adam is connected to sinful humanity. The text is obviously a commentary on Gen. 3, but the Garden, the Woman, the Trees, and the Snake are all eliminated. We are left with a strictly generic account. We will return to a number of these matters in a later chapter.

VII

In summary, Scripture makes a threefold indictment of the human race as universally sinful. Each indictment stands by itself; it need not interlock with the other two indictments. This is nowhere stated in Berkouwer's extensive lectures on sin; nevertheless this seems to be his underlying assumption.

1. Humankind is indicted as sinful *phenomenologically*, i.e., descriptively, objectively according to an accounting of the facts. Of course this is a theologically informed description, for no completely neutral empirical description is possible. This is the method of much of the Old Testament, of Paul in Romans and Ephesians, and of other New Testament authors. The following section on definitions of sin in other religions indicates that every world religion has its own phenomenological description of sin showing that such is the universal state of the race; it is not just a peculiar, biblical view of things.

2. Humankind is indicted as sinful *genetically*. The roots of our sinning go deeper into our past than we can ever trace them. Our Lord indicted the race at the point of the evil heart—a genetic term as we are using it. Ps. 51:5 affirms this indictment, as David traces his waywardness back beyond his childhood memories.

3. Humankind is indicted as sinful *racially*. Rom. 5:12–21 affirms our racial bond without explaining it (along with the materials in 1 Corinthians 15). We are not isolated grains of sand or kernels of wheat or specks of dust. We are one human race. We are biologically and morally one species. All of humanity is either Old Adam or New Adam. We all stem from generic Adam, and we all may be saved by the universal Christ.

No stouter defender of Reformed theology exists in the twentieth century than the Scottish theologian James Orr. In his famous lectures, *The Christian View of God and the World as Centering in the Incarnation*,[14] he clearly affirms that the phenomenological indictment of humanity is the most fundamental:

> . . . it is not rightly put to say that the doctrine of the Fall rests on the third chapter of Genesis. The Christian doctrine of Redemption certainly does not rest on the narrative of Gen. iii, but it rests on the reality of the sin and guilt of the world, which would remain facts though the third chapter of Genesis never had been written. It would be truer to say that I believe in the third chapter of Genesis, or in the essential truth which it contains, because I believe in sin and Redemption than to say that I believe in sin and Redemption because of the story of the Fall (p. 182).

VIII

It is important to examine the doctrine of sin in world religions (Judaism, Islam, Hinduism, Buddhism, Confucianism). Upon inspecting the various doctrines of sin certain generalizations emerge:

1. All religions have a doctrine of sin to explain personal misery, and the suffering people inflict on each other.

2. Christianity has the most well-defined, articulate, and extensive theology of sin. Confucianism resembles Pelagianism, while Islam, like Christianity, takes sin seriously.

3. Only Christianity teaches an articulate doctrine of Original Sin. Other religions believe that humanity is born neutral and may be pushed into good or evil; or else good and evil are equal parts of human nature at birth (a dualism). There is a small similarity in Hinduism to the doctrine of Original Sin in its teaching that each person comes into this world burdened by its ethical behavior in previous incarnations.

4. Linked with a doctrine of sin is the permanence or impermanence of the self. On this score Judaism, Christianity, and Islam have strong doctrines of selfhood. Buddhism considers the self impermanent and therefore takes sin less seriously than the other religions.

5. When the lists of sins defined by world religions are compared, many of the same sins appear on each list. It is the reverse of the theory of natural law. C. S. Lewis attempted to prove the theory of natural law by showing that all religions of the world had the same small number of common positive affirmations. One accomplishes the same thing by pointing out the sins they define in common.

6. Judaism, Christianity, and Islam differ from other world religions in that they postulate a Lord and Creator of the universe, and this affirmation affects their concept of sin. In Confucianism, Hinduism, and Buddhism, sin is defined as going contrary to the cosmic order in a moral sense, as bad habits counter good health in a physiological sense.

7. All religions postulate salvation (although it may never be called that). Insofar as they agree that human beings are sinners (using other words here too), they agree that human beings can find means of escaping misery into a state of happiness.[15]

Gen. 3 does not play the same role in Judaism as in Christianity. There is no doctrine of Original Sin as such in Judaism, but there is a doctrine of the impulse to evil (*yetzer-ha-ra*). This notion is found in such texts as Gen. 6:5, 8:21, Ecc. 15:11–17, 27:5–6, 21:11, Ben Sirach 15:11–17.

All human beings have a primitive drive akin to the Freudian *id* and the Jungian *libido*. It consists of the whole bundle of drives, urges, and pressures with which each baby is born. If left untrained or undisciplined it becomes an evil impulse, the *yetzer-ha-ra*. But there is also the impulse to good—the *yetzer-ha-tov*. If persons are properly instructed in and responsive to the Torah, the *yetzer-ha-tov* will enable them to restrain the *yetzer-ha-ra*.

Sin may be defined in one of two ways. To sin is to go contrary to the Lord and thus break covenant with the Lord and with fellow human beings. Sin may also be defined as going contrary to the Torah, the revealed instructions of God.

In the Islamic faith all is ruled by the one sovereign God or Allah. From this monotheistic standpoint, the chief sin is polytheism. From the perspective of the will of Allah revealed in the Qu'ran, the supreme sin is disobedience to the Qu'ran. However, the Islamic doctrine of sin is actually much more complex. It distinguishes between major sins (polytheism, sorcery, unlawful killing, spoiling possessions of orphans, usury, fleeing from battle, abusing the helpless or faithful) and minor sins. From the standpoint of the sheer sovereignty of God the chief sin is *shirk* or pride (and of course the chief virtue is submission).

Islam accepts the biblical story of Adam and Eve sinning but does not turn it into a doctrine of Original Sin. The course of human depravity seems to rest on two pillars. The first is human weakness to temptations, and the second is the continuous activity of Satan, which does not end until the day of judgment.[16]

The standard by which sin is assessed in Hinduism is *dharma*.

Sin is the transgression of *dharma* viewed as a moral and spiritual law. But sin is not understood in any Christian sense as sin but more as pollution. Each person starts life with a measure of pollution inherited immediately from one's parents and mediately from the previous incarnations. Pollution may arise from ignorance, from specific acts, and from one's death.

Sin is also seen as a sticky, foul substance with which one is born and which one accumulates during a lifetime. Sin is transmitted by physical contact, by speech, and by thought. Even the gods sin.

Hinduism lists more than twenty items that are not in themselves sinful, but that predispose people to sin. The list includes soft couches, dancing, jewels, women, and ill health. Another list, also exceeding twenty, sets out the attitudes leading to sin that are hence called guilt-bearing attitudes (hatred, enmity, pride, glutton, etc.). There are five major sins (murder of a Brahmin, having intercourse with the wife of one's guru, etc.), and seven minor sins.

Redemption is accomplished by purification, penance, sacrifice, and knowledge.

Buddhism is based on six major assumptions: (1) the universe is eternal, not created; (2) suffering is universal; (3) human existence is basically painful; (4) desire is the root of suffering; (5) good and evil are sheer givens and hence beyond philosophical explanation; and (6) the self is impermanent. From such considerations it is obvious that Buddhism has no doctrine of sin in the Christian sense. Nevertheless, listing actions considered wrong yields a list of sins.

Buddhism considers five acts heinous crimes (matricide, patricide, murder of a holy man, wounding in a patricide, and creating schism in an order). It also lists ten immoral actions, four of which parallel the Ten Commandments (killing, stealing, unchastity [adultery], and lying [bearing false witness]). Ten evils (like doubt, pride, ill will, etc.) mar the human path.

Because a human being is a desiring, craving, grasping creature, it invites upon itself suffering and dissatisfaction. Redemption from desiring or craving comes by following an eight-fold path.

Sin has been defined three ways: (1) Not knowing Buddhist teachings, a person sins through ignorance. Each needs instruction from Buddhist scholars. (2) The person sins through delusion or misperception of reality—seeing things in the wrong light. (3) Sin results from being pushed by desire. An unenlightened person may be pressured into sin through desire. This state is compounded by ignorance and misperception. Salvation comes by learning, by knowledge, by enlightenment, and finally by learning how to curb desire.

The summary of secular versions of sin and depravity suggested that the doctrine of sin is not a problem limited to Christian theology. It is universal. Our survey of world religions, as brief as it is, leads to the same conclusion. Christian concern about sin is not a peculiarly Christian problem, although the word sin may not be universally used. The fracturing of the self and the breakdown of society are universal problems. As distasteful as it may appear to secularists, the universal voice of the religions of the world is that something is drastically wrong with the human species at its very root.

4. If Adam Did, How?

I

Irenaeus of Lyons (130–200?) was the church's first genuine theologian. He put together a scheme of redemption in which Adam and Eve are paralleled by Christ and Mary. Adam and Eve ran the course of temptation and failed. Christ and Mary ran the same race under far more trying circumstances and succeeded. This close parallel of Adam and Christ has persisted in the history of theology, receiving a special treatment in the thought of Augustine. None can deny the aesthetic quality of the parallel nor its theological neatness. These are certainly two of the reasons for its strong hold in theology, in addition to such texts as Rom. 5:21–21 and I Cor. 15:20–50. One significant point at which Roman Catholic theology and the theology of the Reformers conjoined is certainly the Adam/Christ parallel.

Another factor reinforcing the traditional understanding of Adam is the notion originating in the patristic period that human history is seven millennia long, in harmony with the seven-day week of creation. This would locate the creation of Adam four millennia before Christ or 4000 B.C. Hence Gen. 2–3 was not only a great theological tract but also an account of the origin of the human race. So Adam was reckoned as any other great person of history. This in turn was reinforced by the work in biblical chronology of James Ussher (1581–1655). The dates he established were inserted into many editions of the English Bible, beginning in the year 1701. His date for the origin of the universe and the creation of humanity was 4004 B.C. John Lightfoot (1602–1675), a famous Old Testament scholar, went even further. He affirmed that the Trinity created Adam 23 October, 9:00 A.M., 4004 B.C.[1]

Further, the New Testament appears to give its *imprimatur* to Adam as a specific historical person of the not-too-distant past in such passages as Luke 3:38, Matt. 19:4–6, Mark 10:6–9, Rom. 5:12–21, 1 Cor. 15:20–50, 2 Cor. 6:16, Eph. 5:31, 1 Cor. 11:7–9, 1 Tim. 2:12–14, Jude 14.

II

John C. Greene gave his book a very symbolic title: *The Death of Adam: Evolution and its Impact on Western Thought.*[2] He meant by the title the end of the understanding of the origin of creation represented by men such as Ussher and Lightfoot and the emergence of new understandings gained from geology, biology, paleontology, and physical anthropology.

In defense of these older scholars, they had no idea of the nature of the world as it is known today. Modern astronomy dates from Galileo Galilei (1554–1642), who first gazed into the night sky with a thirty-power telescope. Further, the great Johannes Kepler lived from 1571–1630, and the genius who put it all together was Sir Isaac Newton (1642–1727). The first real text in geology was published by Charles Lyell (1797–1875) in the years from 1830 to 1833. Although radioactivity of some kind was surmised for a long time, the establishment of radioactive rocks was accomplished in 1896 by Antoine Becquerel (1852–1908). The famous Carbon-14 method dates from 1946, and the sophisticated radiometric dating from the end of World War II.

This means that it was impossible to understand the creation account in the larger framework of things until the twentieth century. Many surmised in former centuries about the vast extent of the space around us and the number of stars, but none of this was scientifically fixed with great precision until the twentieth century. The old dictum that rocks are dated by the fossils and fossils by rocks is no longer true, as geology and paleontology can be developed independently from one other. We therefore have much greater information about the strata of the earth and the fossils found therein.

In 1871 Charles Darwin (1809–1882) wrote *The Descent of Man* and put the human race in the larger framework of the cosmos that all the sciences in consort were creating. Since Darwin, Gen. 1–3 must be seen in the light of modern astronomy, modern geology, modern paleontology, modern biology, and modern physical anthropology.

Modern scientific understandings shake up the traditional understanding of Adam. Therefore, the Second Adam, dependent on the First Adam by analogy, is also shaken up. This disturbs Roman Catholic theology, for its official dogmatic assertions involve statements about Adam, and it likewise disturbs Reformation confessional statements having similar bases. It even more violently shakes fundamentalists who insist on a very literal, very flat historical interpretation of these key chapters.

In the metaphorical language of John Greene, the Old Adam is dead. Both Roman Catholic and Protestant theologians are casting about trying to find a new synthesis with the New Adam of modern science. So it raises the question, "if Adam did, how?"[3]

III

Before we press on to our interpretation of the new or generic Adam we must ask if Adam (in the metaphorical sense) did truly die. This is a serious theological matter, since Adam, the Fall, Original Sin, Total Depravity, the Incarnation, the Cross, the Resurrection, and Salvation are historically speaking all one piece.

First we must make a distinction made by both C. S. Lewis and Huston Smith.[4] Both speak of the distinction between the established scientific data (e.g., dating of rocks, occurrence and sequences of fossils, etc.) and the elaborate speculative theory of evolution that supposedly ties it all together but in fact is not the product of any particular science. Too frequently in controversial materials this distinction is not always observed, which clouds the issues and confuses the debate. On the one hand (1) we have hard data from astronomy and geology that are commonly accepted in the worldwide scientific community. On the other hand (2) we have a comprehensive, speculative, evolutionary theory that attempts to paint a scientific scenario from the original Big Bang to the human race of today. When Christian writers put (1) and (2) together they confuse the debate. If the two realms are fused, such Christian writers feel that anything in realm (1) is wrong because it is built on the evolutionary premise of realm (2), which has never been verified. The scientific creationists attempt to undermine territory (1) (the hard empirical data of geology and palaeontology) by assuming that it is all the product of the evolutionary philosophy of scientists (realm 2).

Furthermore, scientists never escape their humanity. They also have prejudices. Scientists can be dogmatic beyond the facts; they can fudge experiments; and they can make mistakes. No one criticizes scientists as sharply as Paul Feyerabend, an expert in the history and philosophy of science.[5]

1. All geological, paleontological, and archeological work is carried on by a team of experts. The days are long gone when a single person may unearth an artifact or bone, carry it home, speculate about it, and then publish findings as scientific research. All such current work is now the coordinated teamwork of many specialists. One such speciality is *palynology*—the study of seeds, pollens and spores. Within *palynology* is a specialization called *pollen stratigraphy*, which studies the pollen caught in geological strata when they were being formed. Hence scientists know which plants were growing at the time strata were being formed.

2. Astronomy, geology, biology, and paleontology are now carried on in universities all over the world. Scientists with their journals, books, and meetings form a truly international society. The general agreement on basics of the sciences under discussion is close to one hundred percent. If the worldwide scientific community is ninety-nine percent wrong in its assumptions and theories it would be a case of mass deception unprecedented in history. This is not *consensus gentium* ("forty million Frenchmen can't be wrong"), but a case of worldwide "interfacing," communicating group of experts.

3. Science is in a literal sense one science. For purposes of a university curriculum, for necessary specialization, and for the writing of textbooks, sciences are divided into astronomy, physics, chemistry, geology, botany, biology, etc. However, each science may use assumptions, techniques, or theories of any of the other sciences. Experiments with insects or plants or animals on spaceships combine physics (and its theory of gravity) with biology. A

modern physician uses physics to take blood pressure, chemistry in writing out prescriptions, microbiology in dealing with infections, botany in spotting allergies, atomic theory in nuclear medicine, and clinical psychology in working with patients. It would be a most unusual case of mass deception if on all scientific matters the scientific community were correct, but (as the case must be) almost one hundred percent wrong in those matters disturbing the Old Adam. However, the unity of the sciences forbids such an evaluation of the sciences. The same physics that dates the ages of the rocks is the physics that x-rays our bodies, irradiates cancers, and creates tracer chemicals for medical diagnosis.

Our problem then is how to correlate the New Adam with the Christian gospel.[6]

IV

The first and most imperative observation in rethinking the New Adam is that Gensis was written by a Hebrew after the Exodus. Old Testament specialists call Exodus the first book of the Holy Scripture in the sense that all writing of the Old Testament was done by Hebrew authors who wrote within the context of the Hebrew nation that came into existence after the exodus.

An older theory for accounting for the book of Genesis presumes that an oral tradition ran from Adam to Moses. Some sort of linear tradition was affixed to Adam, Seth, Enosh, Enoch, Noah, Abraham, the elders of the Jews in Egypt, and finally Moses. This unbroken tradition is not defensible today for many serious and incontrovertible reasons. This is not to doubt that oral tradition has functioned marvelously among some peoples, as B. Gerhardsson and other Swedish scholars have demonstrated. But attempting to solve the problem of the origin by Gensis by resorting solely to unbroken oral tradition calls for assumptions the theory cannot bear. If modern humanity (*homo sapiens sapiens*) is about thirty thousand or more years old, it is immediately obvious that no oral tradition could have been carried intact over that period of time.

Bruce Vawter, a well-known Roman Catholic Old Testament

scholar, has attempted to deal with the sources that might have been available to the author of Genesis.[7] He lists genealogies, narratives, myths, eteliological stories, epics, and sagas, including all extant materials of the Hebrews themselves.

A Hebrew wrote Genesis after the exodus event with the materials suggested by Vawter. The corollary to this fact is that Genesis is Hebrew history. Traditionally it was presumed that Genesis recorded world history until Terah (Gen. 11:27), the father of Abraham. From that point on the narrative centered on the history of Israel. This reading creates endless critical problems. Beginning with Gen. 1:1, the entire record is Hebrew history. It is the Hebrew version of the manner in which the very specialized history of Israel is connected with creation and world history. Every people on the face of the earth could write a parallel Genesis indicating how their history ties in with creation and world history, and the record would bear the cultural coloring of each people.

The distribution of the materials in Genesis bears this out. Chapters 1–11 are given over to creation and world history while the bulk of the book (chapters 12–50) deals with the history of the patriarchs. On a chapter basis, as many chapters are given to Abraham as are given to creation and world history. Further, the minimum of two thousand years is covered in Gen. 4–11. All of this means that the author sees creation and world history as a necessary preamble to the history of Israel. The preamble is very short in order to get to the important beginnings of the nation of Israel in the call of Abraham.

Two observations may be made of Gen. 4–11. First, it is very highly compacted material, for a few brief pages cover at least 2,000 years. To picture this condensation, imagine a scholar having to summarize the history of Europe from the birth of Christ until today, and limited to around eight pages.

Second, Gen. 4–11 is highly selective. Although it mentions grace and faith here and there, it is mainly about murders (Gen. 4), the wicked people to be judged by the flood, and the defiant people at the Tower of Babel. All of this must be taken into consideration in our understanding of Adam and Gen. 2–3.

V

If the author of Genesis was a Hebrew living after the exodus event, on what basis did he or she write the book of Genesis, particularly Gen. 1–3? The most general answer to this question is, by *divinely inspired reconstruction.*

This problem is far more pressing to Roman Catholic theologians than to Protestants.[8] Official Roman Catholic dogma makes affirmations about Adam and Original Sin that are binding on all faithful Roman Catholics. Therefore, Roman Catholic scholars must correlate their historic faith with modern knowlege; hence the large amount of Roman Catholic literature on the subject. However, Protestants too have been concerned with the issue. The following elements are at the center of the reconstruction theory.

1. Belief that Genesis is part of the divine canon, and that the author of Genesis participated in the grace of divine revelation and divine inspiration with all other authors of Scripture. This means that there is an overarching divine superintendence of the process of reconstruction.

2. In the process of reconstructing the past the author of Genesis made use of whatever materials were at hand. Of course, all that can be garnered from archaeological research has been and is now being investigated.[9]

3. The existence in Israel of a large body of moral materials (for example, the Ten Commandments, the large amount of sermonic and exhortatory materials of Deuteronomy, the very specific ordinances of Exo. 21–23, and the elaborate sacrificial system created to deal with infractions of the covenant) meant that sin was a central concept of the Hebrew mentality. Therefore, we may presume that Hebrews speculated about creation, sin, the nature of sin, and the origin of sin.

Hebrew speculation was very different from Greek speculation at least in form. From a literary standpoint the book of Job is a speculative effort exploring how to suffer wisely if one believes in a God of providence. Ecclesiastes is also speculation. It tries to cor-

relate the many meaningless aspects of life with faith in the God
of Israel. Some suggest that Isa. 14 and Eze. 28 (as believed since
patristic times) are speculations about the origins of sin. From the
human point of view of attempting to account for the materials of
Gen. 1–3, some calculate that the author made use of many speculations in Israel about the origin of sin.

4. Divinely inspired reconstruction is theology by narration.
Gen. 2–3 is unique from the standpoint of literature. It is not ordinary, simple history, for historical science knows nothing of talking serpents, trees with theological significance, or God walking,
working, and talking as the Great Gardener of Eden. It sees God
anthropomorphically. God formed humanity like a potter works
with clay; God planted a garden like a farmer; God breathed into
Adam using lungs; God was heard walking in the garden as if his
steps made noise; and God sewed garments like a tailor. As good
biblical interpretation affirms, anthropomorphisms cannot be tak-
en literally. Yet the church throughout the centuries has read Gen.
2–3 as if it were looking on a literal stage on which these things
were literally happening.

Theology by narration means that theology is being expressed
by telling a story. Theological concepts are in a narrative rather
than being expressed in a didactic style.

Since the late nineteenth century Gen. 2–3 has been labeled a
myth. This was done not only by scholars who had no belief in
divine inspiration of Holy Scripture, but by a number of writers
who were unimpeachably evangelical.[10] At that time there was
only the option of literal history or myth. But in more recent years
the concept of narrative theology has come to fore (I have found
traces of the concept much earlier). Much of Holy Scripture is history out of which theology is derived. The very merging of history
and theology makes it difficult to create a biblical systematic theology. We are using narrative theology rather than treating Gen.
2–3 as myth.

The best interpretation of Gen. 2–3 as theology by narration is
Josef Scharbert's *Prolegomena eines Alttestamentlers zur Erbsündenlehre* ("Prolegomena of an Old Testament Scholar to the Doctrine

of Original Sin").[11] Scharbert admits that Gen. 2–3 is free of theological concepts, abstractions, and technical terms. Yet in narrative form all the major doctrines of the Roman Catholic church
(for Scharbert is a Roman Catholic) about Original Sin appear
there.

Many claim that Gen. 2–3 stands alone in the Old Testament
since none of the other books refer to it at all. Scharbert admits on
the surface this is true. But if one retranslates narrative theology
into customary Old Testament terms the text is very much part of
Hebrew literature. For example, Adam as head of the human race
is Adam as the Stem-Father (*Stammvater*) of all Stem-Fathers.
There is peace (*shalom*) in the Garden until the covenant is broken
and *shalom* is lost.[12]

Karl Barth preferred the word saga. By saga he meant an imaginative literary effort to recover the beginnings of a people. It is a
very specialized form of history, and although scientific historians
may reject the biblical sagas, these sagas are nevertheless a special
form of valid history.

A student once asked Barth if the devil really spoke in Gen. 3.
Barth replied "And have you heard him too?" It was an indirect
response attempting to inform the student that one does not read
sagas like ordinary history. Some special rules exist for interpreting narrative theology or sagas.

1. In narrative theology history is the vehicle, not the literal
message. Of course Gen. 2–3 is an odd text. One cannot read it as
simple history, because then all its anthropomorphisms must be
taken literally. That cannot be done because God has no bodily
parts. Classifying it as a myth has not proven satisfactory either, as
the record reads too much like history to be myth (although in C. S.
Lewis's understanding, a myth may break out into historical form).

2. In narrative theology history is interpreted by the tradition
within which the author writes. This is precisely the genius of
Scharbert's book. This means that the theology behind Gen. 2–3
is to be decoded from the other books of the Old Testament.

3. Theology by narration means that the generic or type is
more important than the individual or person. Gen. 2—3 con-

cerns the generic relationship of the Creator to the human race, the generic relationship of the creature to the creation, and generic temptation. Adam is a generic man, Eve is the generic woman, and the sin is a generic sin.

A famous theological dispute in Holland took place over whether or not Gen. 2–3 was to be read as plain, straight history. The Reformed Church summoned the Synod of Assen (26 January 1926) to advise the church on the matter. Though sturdy Calvinists the Synod refused to make a literal rendering of the passage the orthodox stance.[14]

VI

If Gen. 2–3 is theology by narration it is then generic history. Other terms have been used, such as saga, primal history (*Urgeschichte*), epic, and myth, each attempting to state in its own way that Gen. 2–3 is about reality but in its own unique historical form.

One of the reasons for such a stance is that Adam and Eve are not names like John and Mary. They are generic names. In the Hebrew text the Hebrew word for Adam occurs 562 times.[15] In the bulk of the occurrences it means humanity or humankind. In scarcely more than three instances it means a single person. Eve's name is closer to being a personal name, but it too is a generic name. Eve appears first as the female in the image of God (Gen. 1:27), then as the woman (Gen. 2:22), then as the wife (Gen. 2:25), and then as Eve the mother of all living (3:20). There is generic humankind, Adam. There is also generic male, Adam, and generic female, Eve.

To use modern terms, Adam (the male) and Eve are the generic couple who founded *homo sapiens sapiens*. Huston Smith (*Beyond the Post-Modern Mind*) also wrote *Forgotten Truth: The Primordial Tradition*.[16] Smith spent two decades teaching in one of our major centers of scientific sophistication, Massachusetts Institute of Technology. The experience totally cured him of the positivists' prejudices that only science tells us facts about the universe and that the grandiose theory of cosmic evolution is the only explanation of how it came to be. Instead he suggests something like progressive creationism, which he calls emanation (p. 139). We need not posit all the thousands of connecting links in a continuous chain of evolutionary development. When the world is ready for another specie (or species) God creates it. "The origin of species is metaphysical," is his verdict (p. 139).

Smith does not deny evidence of humanoid species before *homo sapiens sapiens*. *Homo sapiens sapiens* simply appeared in history when God willed it. He uses the term emanation as "the nonanthropomorphic counterpart of special creation" (p. 139).

If the biblical history of Genesis 1–3 is history projected backwards or ideally reconstructed, it must be connected with universal history. The point of connection between Israel's history and universal history is Adam. Adam is, in both the Old and New Testaments, at the same time a generic figure and a person with a proper name. Looking backwards from the point of time at which Genesis was written, Adam stands at the headwater of humanity and therefore of Israel. Reading Gen. 2–3 as narrative theology Adam is a generic person. And so the New Testament can treat Adam the same way. Looking backwards Luke sees Adam as the ultimate ancestor of Jesus Christ (Luke 3:38). In Rom. 5:12–21 Adam is a generic figure, for Paul totally abstracts Adam from Eve, from the Garden, from the Trees, and from the Serpent. Until we learn to read Adam as both a generic figure and the person who in Jewish history is the head of both the Jewish people and the human race, we cannot balance out either the Old or New Testaments.

Holy Scripture was written from an intense Christological viewpoint, as we learn from Rom. 9:1–5 (or the entire three chapters of Rom. (9–11). Christologically, the most important part of all world history is that which began in detail with Abraham (Gen. 12) and came to its climax in the incarnation of God in Jesus Christ—the Second and Last Adam. The events of primal history (Gen. 1–11) are important for the assertions they make regarding creation, the origin of the human race, the origin of sin, and the tragic course of history once sin entered it. But in view of the incarnation, the time span of Gen. 1–11 is relatively unimportant and hence is greatly condensed and compacted. Such concern with particular details and time spans is inspired by a modern research mentality and not by the viewpoint of the biblical salvation-history approach.

VII

What has been said of narrative theology and the generic concepts it yields (generic Adam, generic temptation, generic Fall, etc.) needs to be correlated with the doctrine of sin. Before that is done one more pressing problem awaits discussion. Why believe this generic history? Why not write it all off as interesting Hebrew speculations, nothing more?

Karl Barth from time to time in his great treatise on creation addresses this issue.[17] No theologian in this century has gone into so much detail over so many aspects of the doctrine of creation and the nature of the Genesis narrative as Karl Barth, and none should think themselves prepared to discuss such topics if they have not carefully studied Barth's pages.

According to Barth no one will believe the Genesis narrative if they approach it from only a critical and historical viewpoint. It is a document of revelation, and revelation is recognized and believed only in an act of faith. The historical-critical method may have its place—and does in Barth's interpretation—but it is not and cannot be a substitute for faith.

Nor will any person looking for a typical piece of ordinary factual history believe the account. Barth claims that liberals and fundamentalists have the same version of history. Liberals reject the divine inspiration of Genesis because they do not find scientific history there; fundamentalists accept it because they insist on reading it as if it were a piece of flat historical writing like any other history book.

1. The first reason for believing the text is that it is in the Bible. According to Barth the Bible is the Word of God. It is God's Word among all other words. In this connection he writes: "And it is this

Word, its witness to Jesus Christ, which makes all its words the infallible Word of God" (p. 23).

2. A person becomes a Christian by hearing the Word of the saving gospel of Jesus Christ. Once a person has heard this Word of God spoken in and through Jesus Christ one can hear that Word in other contexts. The doctrine of creation is one of those contexts in which one again hears the Word of God.

3. That which is taught in Gen. 1–3 is in harmony with that which is taught in other parts of Holy Scripture. To believe in Gen. 1–3 is but to believe in the organic unity of Holy Scripture.

4. Agreeing with Calvin, Barth believes in the witness of the Spirit. Just as we are moved by the Holy Spirit to accept the gospel as the Word of God, so by the same Spirit we are moved to accept the creation account as the Word of God (p. 82).

5. If the creation account was written with the great use of imagination, it can be grasped and understood only with a great use of imagination. In this connection Barth wrote: "A man without imagination is more of an invalid than one who lacks only one leg" (p. 91).

In summary:

1. Modern sciences such as astronomy, geology, palaeontology, and related specialties in these sciences have enormously stretched out the time sequences of the universe, the solar system, the appearance of life on the planet, and the human race, requiring Christians to make a new assessment of the method of interpreting the early chapters of the book of Genesis.

2. Genesis is the Hebrew version of the manner in which the Hebrew nation joins creation and the universal history of the human race.

3. Genesis 2–11 must be understood as enormously compacted history and characterized by highly specialized motifs in the selection of materials.

4. Both the Roman Catholic and Protestant scholars who have so courageously wrestled with these chapters understand

them as divinely reconstructed history or as "prophecy in the reverse" (i.e., how the past is recovered).

5. Hebrew speculation of the past and its history in general and origins in particular takes the form of theology by narration or narrative theology.

6. If Genesis 2–3 is understood as narrative theology, it has a far more Old Testament ring to it that previous scholars presumed. It is Scharbert in particular who has taught us how to interpret these chapters as narrative theology and how they connect up with the rest of the Old Testament.

7. In that it is narrative theology the generic is more fundamental than the individual. The interpreter must think first of generic history, generic Adam, generic Eve, and generic sin. However Adam is also the code name of the person who connects up universal history with Hebrew history so that Adam appears not only as a generic person but as an individual in the history of Israel. It is of extreme importance to note how Paul strips Genesis 2–3 down to the generic Adam in I Cor. 15 and Romans 5, omitting all references to specifics in the Old Testament record.

5. The Center of the Theology of Sin

In the following exposition we discuss only those scholars who wish by one means or another to stay in the mainstream of Christian theology, Roman Catholic and Protestant. All who are in this tradition believe that the human race is a fallen race. How and when the race fell remains a matter of great differences of opinion.

The central tradition in the church's theology of sin has been Augustine's view that the Fall was a datable event in history when the original pair disobeyed God and fell from a state of integrity (*status integritatis*) into a state of sin (*status corruptionis*). However, several things have disturbed this view. The first is modern physical anthropology picturing a long human history in which it is either impossible or very difficult to place the Garden of Eden with its original pair. This we called "the death of Adam." A second problem has to do with the concept of *alien guilt*. According to Augustine, Adam's fall plunged the whole race not only into sin, but also into guilt. All who follow Augustine's theology of sin affirm the same.[1] In modern times this affirmation is an acknowledged contradiction. The guilt of one person cannot be imputed to another. The third objection stems from the modern understanding of a free and responsible person. The traditional doctrine violates this in removing sin from the realm of individual will and making it an impersonal force acting upon every generation of humanity.

At least four major conclusions are possible when attempting to retain some notion of Original Sin and the Fall: (1) these doctrines concern the pervasive and powerful social dimensions of sin; (2) Gen. 3 is not about a historic event but is an existential cross section of the act of sin; (3) these doctrines are about the generic roots of sin lying deep within every person; (4) with some adjustment the traditional doctrine can still be maintained.

1. Older liberal theology argued that the real meaning of the Fall and Original Sin is the social dimension of sin and society's power to corrupt its members. Walter Rauschenbusch stated it very simply and clearly in *A Theology for the Social Gospel*.[2] This is essentially the same view as Heinrich Ott who wrote some years later and with greater philosophical sophistication. Ott spoke of an "existential plus" in the concept of sin. This plus factor means that sin cannot be totally defined in terms of personal acts. Original Sin includes both a corporate and universal dimension (pp. 185–87).

From the perspective of the traditional doctrine a symptom (the universal spread of sin) is here equated with the cause as if a disease were not caused by a specific infecting organism but by simply being endemic.

2. Søren Kierkegaard (1813–1855) interpreted Gen. 3 as an existential cross section of the primal act of sinning.[3] His problem with the historic view was that it placed Adam outside of history and the race. None of us begin our lives and our sinning like Adam, yet in the old doctrine Adam is our father in these matters. By interpreting Gen. 3 as an existential analysis of the act of sin Adam is brought back into history and the human race. Adam is our model or archetype in the matter of sin.

This theme, with variations, is the basic approach of Emil Brunner (1889–1966), Paul Tillich (1886–1965), Karl Barth (1886–1968), and Reinhold Niebuhr (1892–1971). It is also the position of a Roman Catholic scholar, Urs Baumann, in his thorough historical and contemporary survey of the problem of Original Sin.[4]

The existential interpretation claims to maintain all the essentials of the historic doctrine but without its problems. It contains a large element of truth. G. C. Berkouwer affirms in his book *Sin* that Original Sin is not only about a past event but also must be our own personal confession (pp. 424–29). We each ratify the deed of Adam. But there is a historical dimension to the Fall that the existential interpretation cannot adequately address.

3. The generic interpretation means that our sin is deeply rooted in human existence. Although we are not sinners in a causal

series from Adam, there is something in our human nature that stems from being embedded in the stream of history and in our own specific communities that predisposes us inevitably to sin. Many instances of the generic interpretation of Original Sin cannot be clearly distinguished from the existential interpretation. Nevertheless, some use a generic interpretation without any specific appeal to existential philosophy.

This view has become very attractive to Roman Catholic theologians, for the dogmatic teachings of the church demand a doctrine of Original Sin. Some Roman Catholic versions of Original Sin as generically rooted are very sophisticated, for example when they speak of "metaphysical immaturity."

As Julius Gross observes, many Roman Catholic theologians interpret Gen. 2–3 as a collection of myths, denying the historic doctrine and opting for some existential version.[5]

Referring to Pope Paul VI who got caught in the cross fire of these debates, Gross writes: "In view of the catastrophic destruction of the edifices of Catholic dogma no wonder Pope Paul VI wailed that the 'church has been shot through with a spirit of self-destruction' " (p. 328).

Karl-Heinz Weger claims that the essence of the Roman Catholic teaching (and apparently all else is negotiable) is ". . . that sin springs from the freedom of men, that it is as old as humanity itself, and it stipulates a pre-personal fallenness into guilt of all men."[6]

Karl Rahner has attempted to hold together the historic dogma and modern learning (and with some sophistication). The Roman Catholic tradition has looked upon Original Sin more as a privation than as an active evil impulse and power. In order to be in harmony with Holy Scripture, Tradition, and Trent one must assert: "A universal solution of the lack of salvation encompassing all men prior to their own personal decision of their freedom, which is history however and not a condition of one's being, which happens through men, and is not simply given through their creaturehood."[7]

Efforts at sophistication of the doctrine are apparent in distinctions made between terms. The real substance of the Roman Catholic faith is *Glaubenswahrheiten* ("truths of the faith"), which may vary their mode of representation: *Aussageweise*. Such a distinction allows many liberties in the interpretation of a text. Or Original Sin is not a historical event (*Geschichte*—history), but it is about our historical existence (*Geschichtlichkeit*—historicality in the existential meaning of the term).

Karl Barth speaks for a number of Protestant and Roman Catholic theologians in taking Adam as the code word for human depravity. (We will deal with his position in a later exposition.) In Rom. 5:12–21 Adam is not a historical person but the sum of the whole sinful human race. The famous text of Ps. 51:5 does not mean that David was born with Original Sin from his mother, but his sinning goes back into the deepest roots of childhood and memory. Thus each of us is an Heir to sin in that we are born into the stream of humanity and history, but each of us is also Originator in that we become sinners as a matter of our personal decision.

In marked contrast to the many derogatory things said of Gen. 3 (especially in the older literature of liberal Christianity), Gottfried Quell has given us a beautiful interpretation of Gen. 3 and Adam in the tradition of the generic interpretation.[8] He interprets the passage as an instructing, informative tract on the nature of sin, the power of temptation, and the dire consequences of sin.[9]

4. A number of Roman Catholic and Protestant scholars accept the traditional formulations with or without making accommodations to modern learning. They argue that matters of a Fall, Original Sin, and Depravity are items of divine revelation and long-standing church confession and are to be received as such. This is essentially the position of Herman Bavinck (1854–1921). He writes:

> Nevertheless, the Fall is the silent hypotheses of the whole Biblical doctrine of sin and redemption; it does not rest only on a few vague passages but forms an indispensable element in the revelation of salvation. The whole contemplation of man and humanity, of Nature and history, of ethical and physical evil, of redemption and the way to obtain it, is connected in Scripture with a Fall, such a Genesis 3 relates to us.[10]

Gen. 1–3 are chapters of pure revelation to Bavinck. They cannot be verified or falsified by science, for they are part of the organism of Holy Scripture. Evolution is still too speculative, too unsure of its findings to present a serious challenge to the traditional view. Further, if a theologian or philosopher rejects the Fall, then sin must be defined as a necessary aspect of creation. This in turn makes God the author of sin.

James Orr has been a sturdy defender of Reformed theology and at the same time a highly informed student of movements in science, biblical criticism, and theology. He maintains that we need not contest science nor engage in running battles with scientists, but that at the crucial points of the Fall, Original Sin, and Depravity we must hold our ground. If these fall the whole Christian system collapses. Redemption in Christ is predicated upon a definite theology of sin, and to undermine the theology of sin undermines redemption and thus the whole Christian system.

C. S. Lewis followed James Orr in time and made some similar points. He devoted a chapter to the Fall in *The Problem of Pain*.[11] First, as a student of literature Lewis claims he does not worry about myth as other Christians do. For example, he believes that the incarnation of God in Christ is the greatest of all myths come true. As a result he has no apprehensions about regarding Gen. 3 as a myth. Myth, he claims, can break into history. He therefore provides his own myth of Adam—his version of how the human race emerged into full humanity in the long historical past. He pictures Adam as a child, an unlearned creature who stumbled into sin rather than having made a considered theological choice. It is an imaginative effort to correlate the traditional belief in a Fall with modern knowledge of proposed human origins.

II

The sophisticated existential reinterpretation and the generic reinterpretation of the Fall and Original Sin run counter to the intention of the meaning of generic Adam. The meaning of this concept is the same whether we refer to Gen. 3 or Rom. 5:12–23. The

Fall does not mean that each person inevitably sins, but that the human race went astray as a race at its headwaters. The Fall is a historical event.

All scholars who work with history or must reflect upon it are faced with the problem of Adam and the Fall. It won't go away. That is why secular versions of Original Sin discussed in chapter two arose. The expression "Original Sin" may be very parochially Christian, but the phenomena to which it refers are as universal as the race is in history and in space. Somewhere, sometime, something happened so that creatures who were once upon a time (if we grant the evolutionary theory at this point) animals, and whose behavior was characterized by animal patterns, began to sin. They began to hate, kill each other, wage wars, and commit every atrocity against one another. The usual assumption is that such behavior was once of survival value, but has unfortunately persisted into the era of civilization, where it has become highly destructive.

This assumption may be true in some instances, but it will hardly carry the full burden. Sinful behavior is sinful behavior and not residual animal behavior. We murder; we rob; we betray. Husbands brutally beat wives. Parents can be cruel and barbarous with children even to the point of maiming them for life or killing them. Adults sexually molest children or engage in child pornography. The drug traffic thrives with everybody involved aware that some of the customers will undergo the hell of addiction. Humans have found endless ways of torturing each other, the very recounting of which can make us retch (for instance, shocking the sexual organs with electric currents or beating the kidneys into pulp with wet towels). An endless stream of violent, brutal, and senseless killings is reported in our papers. Cases of gross sexual perversion move far beyond what might be classed as alternate sexual life styles. Kidnapping exerts maximum sufferings and torture on the parents of a stolen child. Innocent victims are killed irrationally in the strategy of terrorism. And what a list could be made of acts of violence, brutality, and the rawest inhumanity occurring in times of war!

This is not animal behavior. This is sinful behavior. This bears out Pascal's insight that when the noblest of God's creatures (humanity, the glory of creation) deviates from the love and law of the Creator it is then capable of the greatest acts of infamy (humanity, the scum of the universe).

Every person who reflects on human history must question how the human species (again granting the evolutionary theory), emerging out of the animal kingdom, engages in evils far in excess of anything animals do.

The message of the book of Genesis is that this universe exists as God's creation; that the climax and glory of that creation is humanity, male and female, created in the image of God. The beginning of creation is the beginning of history; the beginning of specific human history is also the beginning of sin. Generic Adam is generic sinner. And this means at the beginning of human history is a Fall. That Fall and that Fall alone accounts for the miserable history of the human species. To repeat: the terrible things that human beings do are not residual animal behavior patterns but the sins of fallen creatures.

Again we return to Pascal who said that the doctrine of the Fall and Original Sin is folly to the human mind. It insults it; it threatens to undermine it; it challenges its autonomy; it makes a magisterial accusation. Yet if not granted nothing can be explained; if granted all can be explained.[12]

III

Our concepts of generic Adam, generic Eve, generic temptation, generic Fall, and generic sin follow Paul's mode in handling these texts as reflected in 1 Cor. 15 and Rom. 5. From the Hebrew perspective of history Adam is both a generic figure and a person, and the New Testament treats him both ways; one must not fail to make this distinction.

Understanding these texts generically means that they represent datable historical events. As generic history, or sagas as Karl Barth calls them, they are not the actual history. The relationship of the generic history to the actual history would be similar to the dramatic representation of a crime in a courtroom and the actual crime itself. The two events correspond, but certainly not in a one-on-one, factual sense.

Further, this understanding means that all Adam-speculation is meaningless. Scholars in both the rabbinic and Christian traditions have speculated about Adam's glory and pristine purity coming directly from the hand of God. Others speculate about the immature Adam, the childlike Adam who almost stumbled into sin more than committed it, the Adam of "metaphysical immaturity." In the generic interpretation of Adam this is all meaningless speculation, for generic theology sets out the major assumptions or fundamental assertions of human existence, and hence is abstracted away from all particulars.

If Adam-speculation was one fault of much traditional interpretation, then a second was concentrating on Gen. 3 in a theology of sin to the exclusion of Gen. 4–11. Old Testament scholars today generally assume that Gen. 4–11 is the greatest tract on sin in the Old Testament. Therefore it is wrong to mentally and functionally draw such a fast line at the end of chapter three.[13] In addition, Helmut Thielicke observes in *How the World Began*[14] that the events of Gen. 3–11 are at the same time historical events and typical events. They are typical in that they portray the manner in which sin may erupt in human history again anywhere and any time. Gen. 3 describes sin as a personal affront to God the gracious Lord and Creator. Gen. 4 reveals how sin manifests itself brutally in the most personal relations using the example of murder. Here is the stark irrationality of particular acts of brutality. Gen. 6 portrays sin as a corrupting power that not only reaches to individuals but can become both *endemic* (a disease existing within a population) and *epidemic* (a virulent disease breaking out in a population). Gen. 11 reveals sin as active rebellion of a total culture against God (such as in our day when a government becomes officially atheist in its ideology).

From this perspective it is clear why recent theologians have refused to make such a strong break between Gen. 3 and following material. Concentrating on Gen. 3 overemphasizes the personal dimension of sin and neglects the existence, spread, and power of sin in society, the body politic, and the world at large. The Social Gospel in the earlier part of this century attempted to correct such a personal interpretation of sin with its concept of the kindgom of evil or the kingdom of sin. In the latter part of the century various versions of liberation theology have called attention to the ways sin becomes embedded in the very structures of education, politics, business, and even international relationships. Thielicke's sermons on these chapters in *How the World Began* are both revealing and rewarding.

<h2 style="text-align:center">IV</h2>

One of the standard charges against the traditional interpretation by Genesis (e.g., Augustine, John Calvin) is that Gen. 3 stands by itself in the Old Testament. At best a few later, obscure passages may refer to it. In addition, scholars observe that the rabbis never interpreted Gen. 3 in the way Paul or Augustine or Calvin did. Speculations about Adam and Eve and sin belong strictly to the latest Jewish writings. The charge is then that Paul did not faithfully interpret Gen. 3 but took his cues from the later Jewish literature. What can be said in reply?

This type of thinking led the Roman Catholic Old Testament scholar Josef Scharbert to write *Prolegomena eines Alttestamentlers zur Erbsündenlehre.* Although a relatively small book, it exhibits careful Old Testament scholarship and is full of bibliographical references. Scharbert's thesis briefly stated says that if one takes the traditional terms of the Roman Catholic dogma and rephrases them, reconstructs them in terms of the thought patterns, concepts, and ways of thinking of the Old Testament, one finds no incompatability between the historic Catholic dogma and the teaching of the Old Testament.

His second chapter reviews beliefs about sin held by the people surrounding ancient Israel, showing that concepts of sin and its universality were common in the ancient world. The author of Gen. 3 did not use pure imagination but wrote within a context of common old world understanding. Scharbert concludes his review as follows:

> The above cited texts show us clearly enough that Israel lived in a world in which the thought was not strange that man is from the first moment of his existence a sinner and could "inherit" sin and the destructive consequences, even if only from his nearest direct ancestors. Granted up to this point there are no texts which we could consider genuine parallels to Genesis 2 and 3 (p. 30).

In the following chapters he studies in detail Hebrew words and distinctly Old Testament concepts. For example, the word Adam suggests a wealth of materials in the Old Testament about Stem-Fathers that leads to the concept of Adam as the Stem-Father of the whole human race. Gen. 3 uses only simple, narrative prose but describes the concept of *shalom*—peace, salvation—and the loss of *shalom* in the feeling of shame and guilt. The Old Testament views sin and blessing not as single acts but as powers, forces, and energies. Thus one's sins can ricochet down through the generations just as the blessing of Abraham will eventually reach all the earth.

The Old Testament is full of references to *Erbsünde*, inherited sin. The Old Testament sees a family, clan, tribe, or nation as one vast web of relationships in which events have continuing and interrelated consequences. Dogmaticians and Old Testament scholars alike fail to bring the church's dogmatic statements to life by retranslating them back into Old Testament images. Just as there is an *Unheilsgeschichte* (a history of the loss of salvation), there is also a history of *Heilsgeschichte* (salvation history), and both are based on the Hebrew concept of solidarity or corporate personality.

This is but a small sample of a rich book and a standing challenge to the accusation that the Old Testament is a mute book with reference to the Christian doctrine of sin.

Heinrich Vogel's views on this problem supplement those of Scharbert.[15] According to Vogel it is impossible to understand Gen. 3, Adam, Original Sin, and Depravity until the incarnation, life, and crucifixion of Jesus Christ. Adam's transgression can only be measured in Christ's work. Therefore it would have been meaningless for the Old Testament writers to comment on Adam, so the Old Testament remains silent on the subject. When Christ comes such passages as Rom. 5:12–21 and 1 Cor. 15:20–50 may then be written and understood.

V

The expression "Total Depravity" sounds like an effort to quantify or measure sin. It has often been understood to mean "total corruption." However, if human beings were totally corrupt they would cease to be human. In addition, quantifying moral or spiritual matters is not possible as the expression "Total Depravity" seems to imply.

The expression rather comments on how profoundly sin effects the psyche, and how it affects one's relationship to God. Paul comments on the theme of Total Depravity in Rom. 3:13–18 by using the metaphor of the human body, to say that sin (1) penetrates every part of the psyche so that the whole self participates in sin, and (2) it very profoundly affects the human psyche. Sins may be inspired not only by pleasurable passions, but by the reason and the spirit. Because sin penetrates every faculty of the psyche, there are blue-collar sins, white-collar sins, and sins of the elite.

Certainly the doctrine of Total Depravity does not teach that everyone is as bad as they can possibly be. It simply declares a potential: any given person may under certain circumstances be that bad. Both Fydor Dostoyevsky (1821–1881) and Aleksandr Solzhenitsyn (b. 1918) learned that truth empirically from their experiences in different centuries in Russian prison camps. Every community contains people of good will, people of moral character, people who unselfishly give of their time and energy for the poor or the handicapped or the minorities. The other side of the coin is that a person as sinner is yet to some degree in the image of God. The ratio of depravity to the remaining image of God is absolutely different in each person. The Christian doctrine of sin does not intend to level out such immense differences except on one score: *the mode of salvation.*

Total Depravity translated into the area of salvation means total inability. Paul's whole point in Rom. 1:17–3:20 is a human being's inability on any premises to appear justified before God. This was also the nature of the indictment in Ephesians: Christ is necessary because human beings are sinners. Their sinfulness is measured by their need for Christ. The most moral, ethical, and loving persons yet need the grace of Christ.

The items of Total Depravity, Total Inability, and Concupiscence can be illustrated by the "here-to-there" problem. The "here" represents a one-month-old infant that appears to be a bubble of purity and innocence. The "there" is the same infant twenty years later being charged with a battery of crimes like murder, rape, and theft. The question that the theologian, psychologist, and sociologist must ask is how we go from the "here" of the infant to the "there" of the criminal adult. This is not a fictional example but unfortunately too common an experience.

No doubt there are psychological, psychiatric, and sociological explanations, but, as Stanton E. Samenow discovered in working in depth with more than two hundred criminal cases, these explanations simply don't suffice.[16] After they have been applied to the criminal mind there remains an irrational surd, an inexplicable x-factor, a mysterious unknown. If bad parents produce criminals, why are not all their siblings criminals? If poor communities produce criminals, why are at least ninety percent of those who live in ghettoes or barrios law-abiding? If peer pressure produces criminals, how do some young people escape peer pressure? Why do some criminals come out of the most caring homes?

Most theological explanations of the "here-to-there" problem are inadequate. Too frequently theologians discuss sin in pure abstractions. They omit the demonic, the outrageous, the unbelievably brutal, the horribly sadistic, the immeasurably cruel facets of sin, such as sexual tortures of women prisoners or the unnameable brutalities perpetuated by an invading army upon the conquered population.

Roman Catholic theology usually interprets Original Sin as *privatio* (a lack, a loss, a deficiency), not as *depravatio* (an actual turn towards sin and evil). Original Sin defined as *privatio* is, however, too academic. It cannot account for the aggressive, demonic, sadistic, and devilishly inventive dimension of human sinning. The heart is desperately wicked, not merely deprived.

In his work, *The Ideas of the Fall of Original Sin*, Norman Powell Williams claims that the doctrine of sin was unfortunately formulated by twice-born types (e.g., Augustine or people who have experienced the sordid side of life), not the more normal once-born type (after William James's famous classification) on pp. 154–157. That is an incredibly simplistic statement for such a learned man to make. Any doctrine of sin must explain the most pathological examples of it. Psychology of personality has learned more about human nature from its pathological cases than from normal people. A study of once-born types would never lead us to full or realistic understanding of human depravity.

The only realistic explanation of the "here-to-there" phenomenon is based upon generic Adam, generic Temptation, generic Fall, and generic Sin. Persons are sinners. We are born into this world with potential sinful capacities. How and to what degree they develop or are restrained is part of the unique empirical data of each psyche. Augustine's view of infants, which he saw as depraved, lost, and carriers of total depravity as if they were adults, and many extreme interpretations of it found especially in Protestantism are extreme. One cannot go from "here" to "there" unless the potential of the "there" exists in the "here." That is the meaning of the concept of generic Sin.

The history of the concept of Concupiscence is long and involved. Put simply, it affirms the basic truth that each human being is born with a prejudice to sin. As the Reformers argued, we each have the *fomes*—the tinder, the kindling wood—of sin within us. We need not be taught to sin. These assumptions clarify the "here-to-there" phenomenon.

Only the assumptions of generic Sin and Concupiscence can explain the Scripture texts that speak of profound, radical evil in the human psyche. Psalm 51:5 cannot be watered down to mean that sinning begins far earlier in life than we might expect. That we are

by nature children of wrath (Eph. 2:3) means more than our customary lives are cluttered with big and little sins. The charge that
our hearts are desperately wicked ("more tortuous than all else"),
beyond remedy, and beyond comprehension (Jer. 17:9) certainly
indicates the most profound disturbance of sin at the center of the
psyche.

The Christian cannot and ought not claim too much. Christian
theology has the answer in theory, but only psychologists and perhaps sociologists can fill in the empirical steps. While this potential exists in every human person, the manner and degree of
expression is different for every person. C. S. Lewis suggested that
each person's track record in sin is vectoring out of the original
concuspiscentia in conjunction with the specific pattern of our
lives—our gender, family, race, community, friends, relatives, etc.
Each expresses a unique relationship between generic Sin and the
Relic of the Image of God. The result is an enormous spectrum of
human moral types, from the unspeakably depraved to persons of
great personal integrity, morality, and decency.

One more peg needs to be driven in to support this argument.
Heinrich Vogel in his treatment of sin says that we really cannot
know the origin, depth, and course of sin until the remedy for sin
appears in Jesus Christ and his cross. A vague, shadowy character
haunts Gen. 3 and the entire Old Testament doctrine of sin. We
cannot by the most careful exegesis extract the real doctrine of sin
from these passages. But when Christ comes, prays in the agonies
of Gethsemane, suffers the pains of crucifixion, cries out in dereliction, finally dies, and is buried, then and only then can we really
understand sin.[17] Now we know what Gen. 3 really means; now
we can understand the references to sin in the Old Testament.
Adding to Vogel, now we know the superficiality of Pelagianism,
of the Roman Catholic concept of Original Sin as privation, and of
all other theologies of sin not understood through Jesus Christ, his
sufferings, his cross, and his death.

6. Sin at Its Root

I

Our entire network of social relationships is based on the premise that a person is responsible for what they say and do. The intertwined police, legal, and penal system is built on the premise that people are responsible for their actions. Our entire educational system from kindergarten through postdoctoral studies presumes responsibility. Responsibility is presumed in the less formal and more personal relationships of husbands and wives, parents and children, children among children, and friends among friends.

This means that acts judged good or sinful are free, creative acts of the self. The good act deserves reward because it is freely done. The evil or sinful act deserves censure and punishment because it too is a free creative act.

In more theological language both good acts and sinful acts are the creative, free acts of persons in the image of God. Human social life cannot be conducted upon the grounds of psychological determinism. Whether the determinist is right or wrong is beside the point; rather, the whole fabric of interpersonal relationships is predicated on the assumption that the human person initiates his or her reactions, is therefore responsible for them, and accordingly may be approved or censured.

Søren Kierkegaard (1813–1855) said that sin posits itself.[1] In philosophical language to posit something means to assert something immediate and indemonstrable. It is to make an assumption that cannot be challenged. A sovereign self posits the possibility of both good and evil actions.

Because an act of sin results from the positing of a human person in the image of God, sin can only be confessed and repented of. A person forced to do something cannot take responsibility for it and therefore can neither confess it nor repent of it. Confession is the act of the sovereign self owning up to that which it has posited. If an evil deed can be explained totally as the product of other forces, then it is not sin but a determined act. The emphasis in Scripture that persons can only confess sins and turn from them means that sins are viewed as sovereign acts of the self formed in the image of God.

The other side of the coin is that God forgives sin. If sin posits sinful deeds freely done, then the only manner in which God may respond to confessed sin is to forgive it.

II

Because sin is the free positing of the responsible self, sin is never viewed in Scripture from fatalistic or deterministic perspectives. If we are totally determined chemically, physiologically, psychologically, or sociologically, then the concept of sin evaporates. So also does the concept of truth, for determined things are neither true nor false.

In affirming that people posit their own actions of good or evil, for which they are approved or censured, we do not affirm that such positing is done without a context. The defect in the phrase "free moral agent" is the ambiguity of the word *free*. That is why the above discussion does not include the word. Every action posited, whether good or sinful, is always within a context. The context does not totally determine the positing, and therefore an element of responsibility always remains.

Holy Scripture teaches that powerful spiritual forces affect human beings. Paul writes of contending against "principalities, against powers, against the rulers of this present darkness, against the spiritual hosts of wickedness in the heavenly places" and warns of the flaming darts of the evil one (Eph. 6:12, 16). Peter pictures the adversary of the Christian, the devil, who, roaring out because he is hungry, seeks victims to devour (1 Pet. 5:8). Yet, as G. C. Berkouwer correctly argues, never does Scripture imply that human beings are so compelled by the demonic or satanic that they lose all moral accountability and responsibility.[2]

Holy Scripture also presents human beings as tempted persons. Both the Old and the New Testaments affirm this. Certainly the temptations of Christ at the beginning and at the end of his public ministry represent the maximum possible temptation. Temptations may arise from our inner depravity, or may come to us through sense perceptions, through other human beings, or from the demonic. However, as strong or powerful or seemingly coercive ("peer pressure") as temptation may be, it never eliminates our responsibility if we yield to it.

Holy Scripture recognizes that historical and sociological factors contribute to sin. In this regard Ezek. 18 is a very unusual chapter. There the younger generation declares itself free from the responsibility of its acts because the historical situation is a mess created by their parents. Human history could be defined as one generation having to live in the messes created by previous ones. No doubt there is substance to the claim of the youth. Nevertheless the youth are not absolved from the responsibility remaining with them. This is expressed in the terse line, "the soul that sins shall die" (Ezek. 18:4).

There is a powerful temptation in our times to look at persons as more determined than determining, more as victim than as agent, more as molded than as molder. Psychological, medical, and sociological studies point powerfully in this direction. But a handful of psychiatrists insist that as powerful as these forces are, they never completely determine the individual. A person molded by external forces has already given *primal consent.*

In his book, *Inside the Criminal Mind,* Stanton E. Samenow describes his complete change of mind regarding the nature of the criminal.[3] Criminals are not the total pawns or victims they are assumed to be. On the contrary, they are very responsible persons. A family configuration does not make a person a criminal, for other siblings in the same configuration do not become criminals. Many criminals come from homes with conscientious parenting. Nor does powerful peer pressure make a person a criminal, for there is the prior decision to associate with a given set of peers. Nor do drugs and alcohol make the criminal, for the criminal intent is already there; drugs and alcohol help the criminal commit the crime. Nor do wretched social conditions (barrios, ghettoes) create the criminal, for ninety percent or more of the people who live in such places abide by the law.

Furthermore, a criminal act takes a great deal of thinking. As Samenow comments, criminals are continuously daydreaming about crimes—plotting and planning the next job. Committing a crime takes much planning—how to do it, when to do it, how to escape detection, and the possible escape routes. Most ironic, criminals in their own specialized kind of thinking outsmart all those clever people who think they know how to reform criminals. Criminals have their own shrewd ways of turning all efforts toward reform into service in their own system.

The conclusion one draws from Samenow's studies is that criminals are not pawns, victims, or helpless stooges of all kinds of pressures, but very responsible persons.

Of course Samenow knows that external forces are powerful. Our point is that criminals posit something in themselves that makes the fundamental difference between criminality and law-abidingness. Therefore, no matter how powerful the external forces, there is a strip of responsibility in every such psyche that cannot be negotiated away.

One of the more outspoken psychiatrists of our times, O. Hobart Mowrer, said earlier than Samenow that we cannot dispense with the category of responsibility in psychiatry. Viewing the patient as wholly victim or mentally sick without adding moral overtones or the hint of sin actually worked against the healing of the patient. Among other things, he wrote: "Is every mean or vicious thing that you or I, as ordinary individuals, do not sin but rather an expression of 'illness'? Who could seriously hold that a society could long endure which consistently subscribed to this flaccid doctrine?"[4]

III

One of the themes found throughout biblical revelation is that sin is primarily defined with reference to God. Many formal theological definitions see sin as something contrary to the law of God or a dereliction of one's duty as stated by divine law. Therefore, sin is a relational concept in that it can only be properly defined in the human-to-God relationship.

Categories of sin appear in the world religions. Popular speech includes references to sin. Common sense alerts us to the injurious effects of harmful drugs or poor eating or living habits. The human being as a creature with a sense of moral values cannot but make up lists of virtures and vices. However, in the biblical sense sin is not properly defined until it is defined in relationship to God.

James makes a very important observation in this regard (2:8–11). He comments that if we break one of the Ten Commandments, which one we break is immaterial. To break any of them is to break them all, for it is the same Lord God who spoke them all. This means that to sin is to insult the person of God: the holiness of God, the truth of God, the love of God, the pity of God, the righteousness of God.

The seven penitential psalms (6, 32, 38, 51, 102, 130, 143) express the pure theological nature of sin. However, Ps. 51 is the clearest. "Against thee and thee only, have I sinned, and done that which is evil in thy sight, so that thou are justified in thy sentence and blameless in thy judgment" (v. 4). Tradition assigns this psalm to David and his experience with Bathsheba and her husband Uriah. David is guilty of both murder and adultery. He has sinned against both the husband and the wife. Yet in his lament he says that he has sinned against God. This means that we can never sin against ourselves or our neighbor or community or society or government until we have first sinned against God. In its primary and most fundamental sense, sin violates the perfection of God; and that perfection is the basis for human beings to relate to each other. David had to sin against the holiness and perfection of God before he ever sinned against Bathsheba or Uriah.

Luke's gospel on two occasions repeats the concept of sin as expressed in Ps. 51. The Prodigal Son says, "Father, I have sinned against heaven [God] and you" (15:21). And the publican prays, "God be merciful to me a sinner" (18:13).

This profound sense of having sinned against the perfection of God (including love as well as holiness) distinguishes repentance from remorse (cf. 2 Cor. 7:8–10). The Greek word for repentance means to have a second opinion about something. Our first opinion of sin is our own and it is an approving opinion. When confronted with the perfection of God we form a second opinion about sin, which is God's opinion. Remorse is the sorrow resulting from the problems, alienations, and hurts that come to us in our own sinful lives, but is barren of reference to God.

Augustine was the first to speculate on the ultimate root for sin in the human psyche. He located it in pride—*superbia*. The Latin word means not only pride but also carries the overtones of haughtiness, arrogance, and discourtesy. Although pride and proud have the same Anglo-Saxon root, they are two different concepts. By pride Augustine meant creatures asserting their will over that of God. The essence of the sin of generic Adam was also the generic Sin: humanity determining its *summum bonum*, "supreme good." The closest word in Greek to Augustine's concept is *hybris*, which has several shades of meaning such as defiance of the gods, arrogance, rejection of one's lot in life, haughtiness.

Old Testament scholars agree that the most significant word for sin in the Hebrew language is *pšh*. It is a concept unknown in non-Christian religions. Its root meaning is rebellion, but in the Old Testament it means rebellion against the covenant that the Lord has made with his people of Israel. It is also common knowledge that only in the Old Testament is there a large body of material about the concept of covenant. Covenant hence expresses the most personal kind of relationship between the Lord and Israel but also between the Lord and the individual Israelites. Hence to sin against the covenant is the most wicked form of sin.

It is now becoming clearer why sin is such a serious and central matter. Sin concerns the most fundamental relationships that human beings can have, namely the relationship to their Lord and Creator. But this is also a fundamental spiritual relationship, so that when something interferes with it, all else is changed. Nothing is ever the same.

In his book, *The Great Divorce*, C. S. Lewis makes a very telling point about the seriousness of sin.[5] The greatest thing about human beings is that they are made in the image of God. This Lewis equates with our humanity. The greatest human achievement is then to fulfill, perfect, or realize our full humanity. Therefore, the supreme meaning of heaven is that there we fully achieve our full humanity.

In this context Lewis interprets hell. If heaven is the fullest possible realization of our humanity, then the worst possible thing that can happen to us is to lose our humanity. And so hell is a grubby little English industrial town where people sit behind closed doors and shaded windows as their humanity shrinks to a vanishing point. He ironically pictures Napoleon who even in hell has built himself a vast estate. The irony is that Napoleon will gradually diminish until he is but a shade, a nothing, a vanishing point lost in his vast estate.

This leads to another observation about the seriousness of sin. We sin not only against God but against our own humanity. When we sin we become less than human; we diminish our humanity.

IV

Closely connected with the concept of sin is the concept of temptation. Although scriptural materials on the subject are rich, the literature of theology itself is not.[6] Studies on temptation are usually found in books on spirituality.

Both Hebrew and Greek languages use the same words for testing one's faith as for temptation. The context determines the meaning. Abraham (Gen. 22) and Job are the two classic cases of the testing of faith. When testing a person becomes an enticement to sin it is called temptation.

The structure of temptation is simple even though the modes of temptation may be elaborate. To tempt is to represent an evil as a good. Sin in its true nature may be ugly, brutal, or destructive. In the experience of temptation sin is represented as fun, pleasurable, exciting, rewarding, maturing, or daring—anything but its true nature. In Emile Zola's, (a great French novelist, 1840-1902) novel, *Nana*, Nana does not know that the end result of her yielding to temptations is that she shall die as an ugly black corpse in a bed in some small country inn.

Although temptation may be defined simply, nevertheless it is a very powerful experience. The pressures that can be brought to bear are enormous. The magnets of temptation in the worlds of professional sports, entertainment, and politics makes the head of even the most composed spin.

The scarcity of theological literature on temptation is hard to believe, because temptation is such a central concept for the understanding of sin. Helmut Thielicke includes some good material on the subject in sermonic form in *How the World Began.*[7] Some of the most significant material on the theology of temptation appears in C. S. Lewis's science fiction novel, *Perelandra.*[8] Lewis knew that the intellectuals of Oxford and Cambridge had given up Gen. 3 as a serious commentary on humanity. To write for them a long theological treatise defending the chapter would have been futile. Therefore, he illustrated the basic theological structure behind Gen. 3 in story form to help some of his own generation to take the chapter seriously.

His strategy is to present a rerun of Gen. 3 on the planet Perelandra (Venus). He introduces three characters. The Green Lady represents Eve, the subject of the temptation. The Devil is represented by Professor Weston, and Christianity by Ransom. The substance of the book is the conversations among these three persons. The essence of the book is found in the temptation speeches by Weston, who tries to persuade the Green Lady to see things his way.

The basic thrust of Weston's temptation is that only experienced people can really recognize their *summum bonum.* An innocent, untried person does not have the wisdom from experience and therefore has no idea how to choose wisely. To trust God to lead one is to willfully stay in a state of unprotected innocence. Rather, God wills that we take our own destiny into our own hands, learn through our own experiences, and then choose our *summum bonum.*

There is a large measure of truth in what Weston says. Inexperienced people get seriously hurt in the game of life. Innocence is no protection against scoundrels, deceivers, and tricksters. Experienced people are—other things being equal—more able to pick their way through life than the innocent and inexperienced.

Weston's case is good only if God is not all-wise, all-loving, and all-kind. This good, wise, and loving God has already prescribed for us the *summum bonum*: to love and obey God! The only possible way the Green Lady could follow Weston's advice would be first to disbelieve that God was wise and loving and good and sought only her benediction. We are back to the issue of pride. If the Green Lady decides that she knows out of her own self what her *summum bonum* is then she will act out of pride, for she will have assumed that she knows more of the wisdom of life than God does.

The book includes a richness of interplay between philosophical and theological matters that is not convenient to reproduce here. One other item is worth comment. In the course of the conversations, as Weston grows stronger in his appeal for his case, namely, each person sovereignly declaring his or her own *summum bonum*, he gradually undergoes a change. He more and more becomes the Un-man. This is a carefully chosen word for Lewis. Lewis does not believe that animals have sinned. To call a degenerate human being a beast is both an insult to the beast and a grievous error. Sin has cost Weston his humanity. Sin is not only thinking wrong and doing wrong; sin is degrading one's humanity. The theme in *The Great Divorce* that hell is the progressive loss of our humanity appears here in the image of the Un-man.

We now wish to approach the theology of temptation from an analytic rather than literary perspective. Involved in a theology of temptation are the following propositions:

1. Temptation presumes the complexity of the human psyche. A person is much more than a free moral agent. A person is capable of fantasy, imagination, ambition, pride, and desires for fame. Temptation functions in the center of the richness of the powers of the self. A great deal of the power of temptation—its ability to dazzle or confuse or mentally intoxicate—is due to its operating in the richness of the psyche.

2. Corresponding to the complexity of the psyche in the experience of temptation is the complexity of the context in which temptation takes place. A student who cheats, for example, may be at the center of a pressure cooker. Parents at home expect success. A fraternity or a sorority demands a certain grade average. A scholarship may depend on the grade in the test. Entrance into a graduate program or a professional school may hang on the grade. Peer pressure may exert an influence. Even the student's romantic life might tie into good grades.

Such complex situations face us all. To some the heavy responsibilities of their finances exert enormous pressure in a situation of temptation. For others the pressure comes from the careers or health of their children. Each human being lives in a complex vortex of forces, and temptation occurs within this vortex, making the experience of temptation extremely powerful.

3. In a classic text (1 John 2:15–17) the complex sources of temptation are listed: lust of the flesh, lust of the eyes, and the pride of life. Another famous triad is the world, the flesh, and the devil. All of this means that temptation is not simple. It can arise internally in the sense that a person responds to inner feelings or imaginations or fantasies or exaggerated ego needs. It can also arise externally "from the world." But James 1:14–15 notes that it never comes from God.

4. Temptation is always an indirect approach to the person. This too is part of its complexity. It is rarely an experience in which right and wrong, good and evil, or the truth and lie nakedly face or confront the self. Temptation is seductive, and the very structure of seduction is indirection. When the serpent tells Eve that if she eats of the fruit of the tree she shall be like God (Gen. 3:5) the maximum case of indirection appears. The notion of being like God and making one's own autonomous decision masks the great injury that will come to Eve if she yields to the temptation.

5. Although temptation is so powerful no person ever wins the contest in every situation, it is not irresistible (1 Cor. 10:12–13). The fact that temptation is a daily and powerful experience is reflected in the Lord's Prayer.

"And lead us not into temptation, but deliver us from evil" (Matt. 6:13).

The experience of temptation is different for each person, for temptation is always a test of moral and spiritual strength. A constant theme in novels, dramas, and motion pictures is the ability or inability of people to resist temptation, or the ambiguity the self faces in the experience of temptation. The one point the Christian faith wishes to preserve is that the human person is never totally a victim in the experience of temptation. There is always an edge of responsibility left in each person—large in some, very small in others—that preserves an irreducible element of human responsibility in every moral decision.

This drift toward undermining all sense of moral responsibility caused the psychiatrist Karl Menninger to write his book *Whatever Became of Sin?*[9] with such moral indignation. Menninger knew as a practicing psychiatrist that discussions about sin with a patient would not help but increase the heavy burden of guilt the patient was bearing. This led to the elimination of sin as a proper category of analysis. But he also saw that one could not classify all actions as either neurotic or healthy. Too much was left over unexplained. He therefore argued that sin was still one of the necessary categories to be used in understanding human beings. One must call a spade a spade, and so one must call sin sin. If we don't do this we weaken the ability of the neurotic to regain his or her mental health; and we weaken the resolve of a society to be a just and safe society. Coming from a psychiatrist of such a great reputation the book did prove to be a shocker and very controversial.

V

In a discussion of the theology of sin the question arises about the relationship of Satan and demons to human sinning. Karl Barth has put us all in debt with a thorough review of angelology and demonology in the history of the church.[10]

He affirms that of all the topics of theology this one "is the most remarkable and difficult of all."[11] A survey of the biblical and the-

ological materials certainly bears that out! One of the most difficult aspects in speaking of angels, Satan, and demons is that these
spirits are not a matter of pure biblical revelation in the sense that
they are found in Scripture and only in Scripture. References to
them occur widely in the literature of the cultural worlds of both
the Old and New Testaments.[12]

From patristic times through the period of Protestant orthodoxy
of the seventeenth century the texts on angels, Satan, and demons
were taken literally as part of divine revelation, giving rise to
chapters or sections in theological textbooks on these topics. In
fact, the whole subject matter suffered from imaginative elabora-
tion from St. Antony of Egypt (251?–356) to John Milton (1608–
1674) and his *Paradise Lost*. However, recent Roman Catholic and
Protestant theologians write on the subject with great restraint.

At the time of the Enlightenment the whole realm of angels,
Satan, and demons, was rejected on the basis that such views were
products of prescientific thinking. This became the stance also in
liberal Christian theology. Friedrich Schleiermacher led the way
in saying that the doctrine of Satan no longer had a place in Christian dogmatics.[13]

The stories in the gospels of Jesus casting out demons became a
special problem, for to deny such events seemed to be saying
something against Jesus. The explanation still widely held today
(and virtually an orthodox piece of synoptic criticism) is that these
cases illustrate mental disorders or neurosis and/or psychosis.
Not knowing what psychiatrists know today of mental disorders
they were interpreted according to the demonology current at the
time.

However, this view has been challenged in the twentieth century by both Roman Catholics and Protestants. Missionaries claim
to have experienced true demon possession in their work. J. L. Nevius' (1829–1893) book *Demon Possession and Allied Themes*[14] is
still referred to for its evidence of demon possession based on a
lifetime of work as a missionary in China.

However, the real shocker is the testimony of M. Scott Peck, a
practicing psychiatrist, in his book *People of the Lie*.[15] He describes

two cases in which he is positive a demon was exorcised. He mentions reviewing the entire outline of mental pathology to see if these cases fit into any category of the pathological and they did not. He further states that all other cases brought to him as cases of demon possession he has diagnosed as routine cases of mental pathology. But he claims that after thoroughly reviewing all possible psychiatric explanations in these two cases he found extra symptoms that could only be accounted for by demon possession.

One of the developments in American theology in the 1920s and 1930s is known as *realistic theology*. It was a movement primarily among liberal theologians who realized that their traditional liberal theology of sin was inadequate. Part of this was due to the emerging criticism of religious liberalism by neo-orthodox theologians and partly by the brutal nature of historical events in the first part of the twentieth century. This movement is reviewed by Mary Frances Thelen in her book *Man as Sinner in Contemporary American Realistic Theology*.

Although these chastened liberals did not reinstate the devil they did add the word *demonic* to their vocabulary of sin. The demonic referred to two different kinds of manifestations of sin. First, it meant the kind of mood or atmosphere or spirit that could grip an entire nation. Of course the prime example here is Hitler's Germany. Second, it was used of especially wicked persons whose will to evil appeared far more desperate than that which characterizes the garden variety of sins. Later in the theology of Paul Tillich the demonic receives an even more sophisticated interpretation. Tillich uses the term demonic for three different kinds of phenomena. The great evils which may permeate an entire society as much more than the sum of individual sins are demonic. Tillich also calls the very profound disturbances of the self demonic (and one must remember here that few theologians were so knowledgeable of psychiatry as Tillich). He also has a more philosophical manner of defining the demonic. To him New Being is new life in Christ. Non-being is his philosophical word for sin. That which drives us away from New Being into Non-being is the demonic. Thus, now in the late twentieth century, the demonic is still a viable theological word, if satanic is not.

Hendrikus Berkhof handles the problem of Satan and demons in a different way.[16] He divides theological assertions into four classifications. The first division contains the real, central, authentic teachings of Scripture. The second are those propositions that can be immediately derived from the first division. In the third he puts angels, Satan, and demons. The third division is composed of representations of items in the first two divisions that emerge from the cultural context of the biblical writers but are not binding. Such figures have illustrative but not binding force. According to Berkhof such representations which cannot be taken literally should nevertheless warn us not to take a superficial view of sin and evil in human life.

G. C. Berkouwer takes yet a different approach in his book *Sin* devoting an entire chapter to the demonic.[17] Berkouwer spends no time debating the existence of demons but assumes that they do exist. The thrust of the chapter is that demons or Satan cannot make us sin. The popular saying "the devil made me do it" is pure heresy. Sinners can never escape their guilt by claiming that something in the satanic or demonic realm forced them to sin. Demonic forces may tempt; they can never compel. Therefore sinners remain responsible for their guilt.

Karl Barth and Otto Weber[18] treat the subject in very similar ways. Angels, Satan, and demons are part of the biblical revelation, and therefore one must go along with revelation on these matters. However, the history of the topic has reavealed a crass dualism right in the center of Christian theology. In John Milton's *Paradise Lost* we have Satan pictured as the commander-in-chief, the field marshall of the satanic hosts. Below him are the other greater and lesser generals. Together they function like a kingdom or state and debate policies. Such a picture gives Satan and the demonic an autonomous existence, an existence in their own right. That is sheer and unacceptable dualism.

Barth's argument is long and complex, but the essence of it is (1) to purge out of theology once and for all every possible taint of dualism; (2) to purge out of theology all the speculative accretions that have been heaped upon the subject through the centuries; and (3) to show the completely derivative, subservient, functional role of angels and demons, which in turn defies and resists any systematization. He gives a scant ten pages to demons, stating that one thing they want is attention and that he will not give them.

Weber's treatment is much shorter and is largely influenced by Barth. His main emphasis is that Satan, evil, and sin are sheer givens of biblical revelation. Existing contrary to the will of God, they are irrational, and the irrational cannot be explained. Therefore we must let the mystery of iniquity (2 Thess. 2:7) remain a mystery.

Other biblical texts do not use traditional language of demonology but speak of powers, thrones, principalities, etc. (Rom. 8:38, Eph. 1:21, 3:10, 6:12, Col. 1:16, 2:10, 15, Titus 3:1, 1 Pet. 3:22). Sometimes these are specified without indicating whether they are evil or good. However, Eph. 6:12 is very clear: "For we are not contending against flesh and blood, but against the principalities, against the powers, against the world rulers of this present darkness, against the spiritual hosts of wickedness in the heavenly places."

When Karl Barth visited the United States and responded to questions from the floor he was asked what is the operational or cash value of such texts. He responded that anything, especially in national life, that receives the same kind of response we give to God (loving with all our mind, strength, heart, and soul [cf. Matt. 22:37]) is being influenced by authorities, rulers, principalities, thrones. He cited as examples politics, sex, and sports. T. S. Eliot thought that the kind of response earlier dictators of this century (Stalin, Hitler, Mussolini) received from the populace was a religious, hence demonic, response.

As indicated elsewhere, Ernest Becker is not a Christian writer. But in *Escape from Evil*[19] he argues that whole nations respond to symbols, ideologies, and "charismatic" figures. In other words, evil is not the sum of all the little evils individuals do. There is such a thing as a mass or corporate or national evil. Becker's observations certainly substantiate the concept of evil found in Eph. 6:12.

In the sixth chapter of M. Scott Peck's *People of the Lie*[20] the author investigates the psychology of people who participate in a mass evil. The particular instance was the mass slaying of innocent men, women, and children by American soldiers during the Vietnam War. The parallels with Becker are remarkable. There is a mass instance of evil. Again sin or evil is not the simple addition of all the evils of individuals. There are overarching or superhuman factors in the sense that the evil done is larger than the sum of the individual participants.[21]

A further insight comes from that most neglected theologian Heinrich Vogel.[22] Demon possession is not about the usual imaginative and gruesome representation of a spooky reality. Demon possession is about the inhuman—not the subhuman nor the superhuman nor the human. He says the inspiration behind the death of ten million Germans in World War II is a prime example of the demonically inhuman.

Furthermore, the demonic is not the psychopathic person but the person who is unusually closed in and internally split. There is no immediate evidence for demon possession, only signals that a power is at work in addition to all other possible powers that can influence the psyche. The demonic person does not understand the experience until arriving at the perfect peace of Christ. Only retrospectively from that position can the demonic be understood. Not just a few persons experience this. All Christians who come to their senses, who put on the mind of Christ (cf. 1 Cor. 2:16), realize retrospectiely that they have been possessed to some degree.

Karl Barth, Otto Weber, and presumably Heinrich Vogel would affirm that angels and demons do not have autonomous existence. They serve only functionary roles and therefore are at the edge or in the shadows of theology. The three theologians are correct in affirming that if we accept Scripture as divine revelation we must go along with the corpus of revelation that speaks of angels and demons and not attempt to portion revelation out into acceptable and unacceptable pieces.

VI

In Christian theology sin is not an autonomous concept. It is a concept that has no meaning outside of such concepts as God, holiness, justice, love, and purity. Furthermore it is not a focal concept. The Christian faith is concerned with sin because there is a gospel. When the Christian faith discusses sin apart from gospel it invariably gives the appearance of a moralism at best and a hypocrisy at worst. It is very difficult to attack sins, injustices, or violence as such and avoid distortions. Discussions of morality or justice apart from the gospel distort the Christian message into humanitarianism. They give the impression that Christians are the graceless monitors of public morality, turning Christianity into a religion of morals and not gospel. Karl Barth's method of handling this dilemma was never to speak to labor union meetings without mentioning Jesus Christ and never to preach the gospel in the church without mentioning social problems.

The gospel is good news to sinners. This presumes that a person must have some sense of his or her sinfulness to be interested in the gospel. One of the standard items in the doctrine of salvation is the conviction of sin. The question is then, how in preaching is the consciousness of the listeners to be aroused about one's sinfulness? How does the preacher lead a person to the publican's prayer, "God be merciful to me, a sinner"?

The first part of this problem in preaching is that it is one sinner (the preacher) telling another sinner (the listener) about sinfulness. How can this be done without looking like bald-faced, open hypocrisy? If it is not done how shall there be faith? We must find the right "existential distance" between the preacher and the listener. The preacher must come close enough to the listener so that the conscience is reached but not close enough as if the preacher were prying behind closed doors. No one can measure this existential distance, for it is a matter of the wisdom and taste of the preacher as well as the preacher's regard for the personal integrity and worth of every listener.

The second part of the problem of evoking a sense of need or sin with respect to the gospel is the content of such preaching. Here the scope is rather large. So much traditional preaching has been based on a law/gospel motif. If by the law is the knowledge of sin then preaching of the law ought to raise the level of the consciousness of sin. A sermon is then divided into two parts. The first part is occupied with the preaching of the law to create a sense of sin, and the second part is devoted to the remedy of sin in the gospel.

The truth of the matter is that all of the methods we shall discuss have worked. The law/gospel motif has been very successful. However, it also has some limitations. It presumes that the audience is half-converted. That means that the listeners already have a grasp of the fundamentals of the law. They are in the Christian tradition. It also presumes a connection that might not exist, namely, that preaching the law automatically raises one's consciousness of sin.

Another method of attempting to raise the consciousness of sin is to center on the daily failings, errors, foibles, and weaknesses of the listeners. Concentrating on personal shortcomings has a high degree of relevance. The preacher is not applying some abstract concept as law but whittling away at the specific known failings of the listener. But this approach has its problems, too. It is based upon the preacher prying into the personal lives of the parishioners. The preacher wants this diagnosis of sin to proceed in one direction; namely from the preacher to the parishioner. The preacher has no intention of asking the parishioners to pry into his or her private life. But there is also a deeper theological issue. Our real sinnerhood is not perceived in our daily foibles and failings. We begin to grasp the real depth of sin when we speak of coming short of the glory of God.

In recent times the "apocalyptic shakedown" has been used. We now can envision global failures or catastrophes. We could so poison our world, ecologically speaking, that life could become impossible. World population could exhaust world food production. There may be atomic blackmail and worst of all nuclear war. By shaking up the stability of the whole world the preacher hopes to shake up the sense of stability in the listener. Pragmatically it works, but it raises a serious question in Christian ethics whether such scare techniques are ethically proper.

Much more prevalent is the psychological shakedown. This

technique focuses on the failures of life: failures in occupation, failures in marriage, failures in coping with alcohol or drugs, failures in raising children. It may focus on psychological problems such as excessive guilt feelings, depressions, or a lack of a healthy self-image. Of course this too has an immense practical relevance and in many instances has had much success. The searching question to be asked is whether this is precisely what is meant in the New Testament by the conviction of sin.

More philosophical and reflective is the existential method pioneered by Søren Kierkegaard. This method attempts to show that an entire life is misaligned. The entire scope of one's life is out of focus. This method has been used differently by Paul Tillich and Helmut Thielicke. Paul Tillich is more philosophical and abstract in his presentation than Thielecke, but his aim is to show that if one looks at sin through existential eyes (or categories), one sees that the essence of sin is total existential misalignment of one's mode of living and thinking. Helmut Thielicke depends more on picking up stories in the Gospels and showing how the particular person's failure in life can be explained best from a popular existential standpoint. The existential analysis of sin does come closer to the core of the problem than some of the other methods we have mentioned.

Karl Barth has attempted to prove that the real, valid, scriptural consciousness of sin is achieved through the preaching of Christ and the gospel. If Jesus Christ is God's True Human, if he is the incarnation of the ideal human, if his nature is the model human nature, then the true sense of a person's sinfulness will arise if one preaches Jesus Christ. Of course this is a very positive and inspirational manner of reaching the sinner.

From the sheer pragmatics of preaching (as already indicated) all methods have had good results. Each method is only as good as the character of the preacher. Whatever the strategy of the preacher, it must be theologically sound; it must respect the rights of the listener; it should not be justified on the sheer pragmatism of success; and no matter how successful in the shorter vision, it should prove healthy in the longer vision.

VII

We are omitting a detailed study of Hebrew and Greek words for sin, as that is the territory of specialists. The standard work on Old Testament words for sin is that of R. Knierim.[23] An extensive article in the *Theological Dictionary of the New Testament*[24] reviews the words of the Old Testament but does not deal with all the New Testament words for sin. S. J. de Vries has a most comprehensive and highly valuable article on sin in *The Interpreter's Dictionary of Bible*, which combines lexical and theological materials.[25]

One observation is in order. Linguists have amply warned of the dangers in the attempt to assess meanings of words from a study of their etymology or roots. People may understand words very well without knowing of their derivation. In many instances the current meaning of a word has drifted far from its original context. Thus all purely lexical studies of words for sin face this limitation.

VIII

After reviewing the theological history of the concept of sin, Paul Jacobs summarizes the biblical elements in a doctrine of sin.

Sin is primarily a power. As a power it is at work in the personal lives of people and in the larger social units. It therefore cannot be adequately defined as a privation or a deficiency. It is an immanent power in that in any situation in a person's life sinning is a possibility. It is a transcendental power in that it may manifest itself in the decisions or actions of larger groups from the local community to the state itself.

As powerful as sin may be it is never greater than the power of God. According to the biblical materials, God holds sin in check and within limits. In grace and salvation God can reverse the effects of sin. Although one could say that sin and grace are polar opposites there is no doubt in Scripture that grace has the greater power. Otherwise there would be an unacceptable dualism.

Sin is a pervasive power. It can penetrate into the depths of the self and so be intensely personal. But is also is an effective power in the total range of humanity. This is the functional meaning of the doctrine of original sin.

Sin always points in two directions. Each sin points towards God and humanity at the same time. If someone steals something that person has transgressed the law of God and that points the sin upward towards God. But in that it is an earthly deed against one's neighbor it points towards humanity.

We cannot totally define or explain sin in terms of purely human experience or purely as a sociological phenomenon. Sin can only be sharply defined in terms of its transcendental dimension, i.e., it is a sin against God or it is a sin against Christ or it is unbelief before the law of God.

7. The Consequences of Sin

Scripture everywhere assumes that a person's deeds have effects. Paul calls it the law of sowing and reaping (Gal. 6:7–10). The first effect is upon the sinner. Evil deeds tend to make the person more evil, and good deeds make the doer more just. The second effect concerns consequences. Sinful deeds lead to doleful consequences, and good deeds lead to a more blessed life. Sin has consequences in both senses.

1. The first consequence of sin is to evoke the wrath of God. The thought here is not complex or involved. A God of perfect holiness can have only one assessment of a sinful act and that is to judge it wrong. The literature on the wrath of God is both large and controversial.[1] However, without rehearsing the story of its treatment in the history of theology, two texts of Scripture suffice here.

In indicting the Gentile world for its sinfulness in the book of Ephesians, Paul sums up his case by calling both Jews and Gentiles children of wrath (Eph. 2:3). In the Hebrew mode of speaking, when a person is preeminently characterized by something they are called a child or son of that characterization. Hence to be children of wrath means preeminently to be worthy of wrath. How the wrath or holiness of God is related to and functions with the love of God has been debated with various formulations from Martin Luther to Karl Barth. None of that debate alters the affirmation of the text that the consequence of sinning is to make a person a child of wrath.

However, Rom. 3:19 sets the issue beyond debate. Paul's purpose from Rom. 1:18 to 3:19 is to prove that the whole world is accountable to God for its sin. When in 3:19 Paul says that every mouth is stopped he means the person so charged has *absolutely* no case. The person stands unquestionably guilty of the accusation. Then Paul adds that the entire world is accountable to God. He uses the word *hypodikos*, which means liable to the judgment of the crime involved.[2] Some have suggested (and perhaps rightly so) that Paul does not use stronger language here for in immediately introducing salvation through Christ he means to suggest that the case is not hopeless.

2. The New Testament speaks of sinners as being lost. The concept of lostness comes to its clearest expression in the three parables (or one parable in three versions) of Luke 15 (lost sheep, lost coin, lost son). Involved in the concept of lostness are the notions of wandering and destruction. Sinners are lost in the sense that they have wandered from the purposes and will of God. Lostness also implies the possibility of being destroyed. To be lost is to be lost to God, to oneself, and to the kingdom of God and its purposes. As the parable of the Prodigal Son shows, willful sin produces this lostness.

3. Sin produces alienation. In a remarkably compact paragraph Paul identifies sinners as being ungodly, weak, and enemies (Rom. 5:6–10). Furthermore, the great chapter on divine reconciliation (2 Cor. 5) presumes the enmity of the sinner, for the function of reconciliation is to remove enmity. Enmity refers to the state of hostility that has the potential of breaking out into war. Sin produces this state of enmity or hostility or alienation. It is so profound that it is only removed by the sufferings and death of the cross of Jesus Christ.

4. Sin also produces spiritual death (Eph. 2:1–3). In a number of texts death is used metaphorically to describe a kind of spiritual existence (Rom. 7:10, 8:6, etc.). Spiritual death can mean that no positive lines of spiritual communication exist, as well as being insensitive to spiritual realities.

II

Roman Catholics, eastern Orthodoxy, and Protestants all have agreed that one of the wages of sin is physiological death. Adam is warned of death in Gen. 2:17. Upon sinning he is sentenced to biological death (Gen. 3:19). The New Testament confirms this interpretation in the famous passage of Rom. 5:12–21. Adam and Eve were created immortal or potentially immortal if obedient;

but their sinning interrupted this potential immortality and brought the sentence of death.

As long as theologians reckoned humankind's existence on this earth as not more than six thousand years and interpreted Gen. 2–3 in a literalistic and historical sense, the above interpretation appeared unchallenged. With the progressive development of geological science, paleontology, and physical anthropology (which includes fossil remains of the human species), this traditional interpretation came under both challenge and scrutiny. The crust of the earth has been the graveyard of fossils bearing witness to literally millions of living creatures who have died. As far as the fossil record is concerned, death has reigned as long as there has been life on the earth. The fossils of trilobites have been found in abundance in Cambrian rocks dated some 570 million years ago.

From the same crust of the earth have come the fossils of humans or prehumans (however one wishes to label them). The movement from Australopithecus to Homo Erectus to Neanderthal (Homo Sapiens) to Modern Human (Homo Sapiens Sapiens) covered at least a half million years. Modern humanity first appeared some thirty to thirty-five thousand years ago. All of these prehumans or humans have died, been buried, and some have been fossilized. So the question arises if it is possible to believe that biological death came to Adam and Eve some thousands of years ago and passed upon the present human species.

Another observation follows. All complex organisms pass naturally through a cycle from birth to youth, adulthood, old age, and death. Organisms do not live immortally but wear out, and the processes of humans wearing out is no different from the other organisms, even though humans are among the longest living organisms. If the processes of rebuilding (anabolic) were equal to the processes of wearing out (katabolic) an organism would continuously live, but no such organism is known.

This increased knowledge of fossils and of the nature of living organisms has sent theologians back to the Holy Scriptures to see if the texts actually teach the historic understanding of the texts. Does Gen. 2–3 actually teach the potential immortality of Adam and Eve? When Paul speaks of sin and death does he literally mean biological death?

Theologians have broken into two camps over this issue. The first contains those who retain the traditional doctrine that physiological death is the result of sin. They take this meaning from Rom. 5:12 and confess it as a matter of divine revelation. The evidence of fossil records and our biological knowledge of human death are disturbing considerations, yet the connection in divine revelation between sin and biological death cannot be severed. They list further proofs of the connection between sin and biological death: Jesus Christ had to suffer death itself for our sins; humankind's worst enemy is death; and our redemption includes our own bodily resurrection.

James Orr argues that since we do not know what Adam and Eve were like in their innocence, we have no way of assessing their special physiological state. Therefore the current knowledge about our bodily death does not bear on the question.[3]

C. E. B. Cranfield had to face the number of texts in the book of Romans which apparently connect sin and biological death. In a special note on the matter he comments on the problem as introduced by modern medical science. In this connection he writes:

> It is not necessarily obscurantist to believe that at the point (or, maybe, points) at which man first appeared as recognizably man he was faced with, but rejected, a God-given possibility of, and a God-given summons to, a human life such as did not need to be terminated by the death which we know, that is, a death which is for all men objectively (according to the witness of Scripture) death-as-the-wages of sin, whether or not they subjectively know it as such.[4]

He concludes with an observation made by most commentators on the relationship of sin and death: whatever may be obscure in Scripture on this point, or whatever difficulties modern knowledge may create about the subject, the whole issue is clarified by the death and resurrection of Jesus Christ. As a consequence of that event our own resurrection of the body is assured.

The second camp is made up of both Roman Catholic[5] and Protestant theologians who believe biological death is a natural process and science cannot be contradicted on this point. The outstanding Lutheran theologian Paul Althaus declares that the description of the First Adam in 1 Cor. 15:21–22, 42–50 is definitive teaching for Christian theology. He claims that that passage teaches that Adam was created a mortal creature to whom death came as a natural event.[6]

Others in this second camp argue that generic Adam and generic Eve were created mortal. If they had not sinned they would have died a death of peaceful transition from this life to another. In fact, Scripture records a number of such peaceful transitions.[7]

However, the act of sin is an act of death. It is the willful separation of the creature from the Creator. The result is that all the fear, shame, horror, and guilt that sin produces in the sinner becomes centered in (1) the prospect of biological death and (2) even in the event itself. Biological death, in threat and reality, has now become to the sinner a fearful eschatological experience. Representing this new consensus are Helmut Thielicke, Eberhard Jüngel, Otto Weber, Karl Barth, Emil Brunner, and the Roman Catholic theologian Karl Rahner.[8]

No author has captured so well the fear of the experience of dying as Leo Tolstoy in *The Death of Ivan Ilyich*.[9] Ivan screamed incessantly for three days before he died. Ernest Becker argues in *The Denial of Death* that no person domiciles death.[10] All forms of apparent peaceful reconciliation to death are but the subterfuges of the unconscious in its unrelievable fear of death. Added to this new consensus as partial substantiation have been the reflections on death by the existentialist philosophers Martin Heidegger (1889–1976) and Jean-Paul Sartre (1905–1980).

The Lutheran theologian and accomplished preacher Helmut Thielicke has given an eloquent, passionate, and unforgettable sermon on death as seen in this second camp (and it is a memorable sermon for those who remain in the first camp). He shows in a painful but telling way that once a person is a sinner, death can never be only a natural or biological event. He agrees with Becker that the human person can never reconcile death to him or herself as a natural event; not even the medical profession, which daily lives with it, can do this. But as a Christian (which Becker was not) Thielicke points out that Jesus Christ in his resurrection and in his gospel take the sting out of the event of biological death.[11]

III

When Paul commented on Gen. 3 in Rom. 5:12–21 he abstracted all the details away and presented us with the sheer fact of the person of Adam and the event of disobedience, giving the impression that all else was historical and geographical trimming. He does the same thing with the pronounced curse of Gen. 3:15 in Rom. 8:18–26. He ignores the toil, thorns, thistles, and sweat and concentrates on the one solitary fact of the misery of human existence as the consequence of sin.

What point is the apostle making? The famous Dutch Calvinist, Abraham Kuyper (1837–1920) put his finger on the issue when he wrote, "Psyche, body and world form together one organic world."[12] He meant that what happens to the self cannot but have a repercussion on the body, which in turn cannot but have a repercussion on the cosmos in which the body exists. There is an organic connection between psyche, body, and cosmos. On the event of sinning, the soul spiritually dies; this in turn anticipates the return of the body to dust; this in turn speaks of the curse in the cosmos in which the body lives.

The same point is made by James Denney in commenting on this text in Romans when he wrote, "[Paul] conceives all of creation as involved in the fortunes of humanity but this . . . naturally leads to the idea of a mysterious sympathy between the world and man. . . . Creation is not an inert, utterly unspiritual alien to our life and hopes. It is the natural ally of our souls.[13]

For sufferings Paul uses the Greek word *pathemata*. It means all the sufferings in this cosmos that are in the inevitable consequences of human sinning. It is the sufferings, as he identifies them, *of this present age*, which is the age prior to the messianic victory.

These *pathemata* introduce into our experience vanity or emptiness or events completely opaque in their significance, events of futility, frustration, or disappointment. The guilty pair is ejected from the Garden, the Paradise, and must now suffer the conditions under which all other life is lived. In commenting on the Genesis text H. E. Ryle says that the curse and its effects "are not new products of the soil because of sin, but are typical of that which the earth brings forth itself, and of ground neglected or rendered fallow by man's indolence."[14]

Existence for the disobedient pair is no longer Edenidyllic. Their lives must now be carried on under the identical conditions of all other living creatures. The divine purpose—*telos*—is frustrated by sin. The apostle Paul's point is that the Christian lives under the identical conditions. Faith in Christ, justification and salvation bring no exemptions. To block the *telos* of existence is to also inhibit the freedom (*eleutheria*) that rightfully belongs to the children of God. The law of existence, which is the bondage to decay, applies equally to Christians. The final verdict of such existence is death (1 Cor. 15:26). Hence all life—Christian and non-Christian—is lived under the conditions of suffering (*pathemata*), futility (*matainotes*), or the frustration of the divine purpose (*telos*), bondage (*douleia*), and weakness (*asthenia*). This is all so very realistic, so very accurate, so very true to the daily life of Christian and non-Christian. We all experience the bounty of nature but also its death-dealing catastrophes. We enjoy the thrill of being alive only to be interrupted by some senseless death.

According to Kuyper's logic (which we think is in harmony with sacred Scripture) a psyche that sins can exist only in a body upon which the verdict of death has been passed; this body in turn can live only in a cosmos upon which a verdict of the curse has been passed.

IV

The status of children who die in their infancy has been debated the entire history of the church.[15] Essentially the question is whether the rules or conditions that apply to adults also apply to infants, or whether infants constitute a separate class. The question also includes all persons who never reach the age of account-ability (a flexible concept at best), such as the mentally defective and retarded. Are children who die in infancy (and all other re-tarded persons) reckoned as sinners and in need of grace, or do they die in a state of innocence and so are a special instance?

The famous British Baptist preacher, Charles Spurgeon, (1834–1892) collected in a sermon all possible references to the status of children dying in infancy, but as enticing as some of the references are, there is no clear scriptural teaching.[16]

The earliest Christian tradition is apparently that children of Christians are Christian and have the right to Christian baptism. The precise early Christian practice about the baptism of infants has been debated in recent years by Joachim Jeremias (who argues for a very early date of the practice) and Kurt Aland (who argues for a date a couple of centuries later).[17]

Cyprian (d. 258) and Augustine (354–430) argued that infants were sinners and therefore needed Christian baptism. Others, such as Gregory Nizianzen (329–389) and Ambrose (339–397), agreed. However, Roman Catholic theologians of the Middle Ages developed the doctrine of a special place for such infants called the *limbus infantium*. This is a place free from either the bliss of heaven or the pain of hell. This teaching never reached the status of official Roman Catholic doctrine.

Ulrich Zwingli (1484–1531) suggested that all children dying in infancy were elect, and he has been followed by many Calvin-ists. Others base the salvation of such infants on their relative in-nocence; others on the belief that the first vision of such infants in the world to come is Jesus Christ, in whom the infants in their in-nocence immediately believe; and others on the wonderful mercy of God. If we err let us err on the side of the mercy of God and include all such persons within the redemptive purposes of God.

V

Some of the strongest lines ever penned in the history of theol-ogy outlining human depravity are those of John Calvin.[18] Some have accused Calvin of teaching that human beings are so totally corrupt that they cease to be human. However, this overlooks Calvin's doctrine of common grace[19] and his discussion stemming from that concept. Calvin's notion of a general grace of God (known as common grace in the Calvinistic tradition) is his observation that humankind is not totally degenerate; otherwise there could be no art, sciences, learning, or society. It is therefore necessary to balance Calvin's view of humanity's total depravity with his commentary on general or common grace.

In Calvin's own words, a *residue* of the image of God remains in the fallen sinner. Sin corrupts the image of God but does not destroy it. In human reason "some sparks still gleam" (par. 12). Nor did the human will perish in the fall. There remains in the breast of every person an appetite for truth, which sin does not annihilate. Human beings as social creatures also have implanted in them a respect for law, which sin has not dampened. In this connection he remarks, "Yet the fact remains that some seed of political order has been implanted in all men. And this is ample proof that in the arrangement of this life no man is without the light of reason" (par. 13).

Next Calvin turns to art and science and says that the ability to perform in these territories is due to a talent inborn in human nature. The Fall did not reduce humanity to subhuman creatures, evident in the fact that both the impious and the pious have skills. The light of God's truth shines upon the minds of unregenerate people enabling them to make accomplishments in the arts and sciences. Though unregenerate they are ornamented with God's excellent gifts. Any gift in the form of a talent is a gift of the Holy Spirit, and therefore to despise gifts in the impious is to despise the Holy Spirit. Examples of such unregenerate people gifted by the Holy Spirit are the ancient (pre-Christian) jurists, philosophers, medical scientists, and the poets. He concludes this observation by remarking that God has left over to the human psyche many good gifts even though the race is plunged in sin.

The Holy Spirit works in the Christian and non-Christian alike so that it is the Holy Spirit who guides all in "physics, dialectic, mathematics, and other like disciplines" (par. 16).

Christians who neglect such arts are neglecting the gifts of God and are therefore guilty of sloth. Whatever order, law, science, progress, or arts exist are due to the preserving and inspiring presence of general grace. "Still, we see in this diversity [of gifts] some remaining traces of the image of God, which distinguish the entire race from the other creatures" (par. 17).

Calvin's concept of general or common grace, along with his concept of the relic or the image of God in the sinner helps us explain humanity as (in Pascal's terms) the glory and the scum of the universe. In that we still retain some glory in the relic of the image of God, unregenerate humanity is capable of great art, great science, great literature, and great political leadership. In that we are also scum we are capable of endless deeds of infamy, crime, treachery, and degeneracy.

In a general way Karl Barth stands in the Augustinian-Calvinistic tradition on the subject of the doctrine of sin. He calls attention to the predicament we would be in if we were totally worthless and hated of God, as some of the strong Calvinistic language has asserted. If that were true, God would not love us, nor would Christ die for us. We would not be worth saving. Therefore, beneath the rubble of sin must be an essentially good human nature, which God can love and can save. This is said by a theologian who had no sympathies with Pelagian views of sin.[20]

VI

Since the Enlightenment of the eighteenth century, the concept of progress has become a major category in philosophical, sociological, theological, and scientific discussions. It has become a *Kampfparole*—a category surrounded by contention. Does the Christian doctrine of sin have any relevance in the discussion of the concept of progress?

The idea of progress is as old as the Greeks and as modern as the latest journals.[21] However, discussions on the topic are frustrating because disagreement exists on whether the topic can be meaningfully discussed without definition and whether it is possible to define the term.[22]

On certain levels the answer is clear. There is progress in the speed of transportation. There is progress in eliminating plagues and epidemics. There is progress in extending the life of persons— at least in Western countries. There is progress in universal education. There is progress in medicine and pharmaceuticals.

However, the issue becomes much more confused if we ask if the psychological state of people is improved. Do people feel happier? Is there more joy in their lives? Are they freer from crime within and wars without? Do they die in a greater state of contentment?

Henrikus Berkhof responds to the question by dividing it in two and indicating those territories where he thinks there has been progress, and those about which he has questions. In the latter class he lists art, the human ethos, love, empathy, and religion.[23] Our concern is with that latter classification because that is where the concept of sin is more relevant.

It is common to divide the opinions on the idea of progress into three groups: the *meliorists* believe that progress is possible but not automatic or inevitable. It results from intelligent planning and forceful exercise of the will. The *utopians* believe that progress is inevitable, although it may not be an unbroken upward rising line. Reverses are possible, but the drift is always upward. The *pessimists* believe that there is no progress although there may be periods of advances and improvements, but there is also the possibility of radical reversal. Christians may be found in all three groups, for a good number of theologians and ethicists believe it is both a Christian mandate and an actual possibility to improve the lot of humanity. There have also been Christian *utopians* of many sorts especially the older version of postmillennialism. The Augustinian tradition in Christian theology has fallen clearly in the pessimistic camp.

The last chapter of Nisbet's book is entitled, "Progress at Bay."[24] It is a very valuable chapter because he not only explains why the twentieth century has cast such doubts on the notion of inevitable progress, but he also gives a historical review of scholars, philosophers, and historians who warned against optimistic assumptions about progress. One can agree with Nisbet and even say something more from the Christian perspective. Nisbet's statement might be called commentary on the doctrine of sin. And certainly the Christian doctrine of sin suggests pessimism rather than optimism. The following is how I would supplement Nisbet's description by adding to it the insights from the Christian doctrine of sin.

(1) The growth of totalitarian states (Marxists and militaristic versions) in which the values of a free society are severely controlled by force and imprisonment; (2) the capitalistic-technological society creating modes of living that systematically destroy the healthy factors of a culture; (3) the continuous ecological contamination of our planet, either eventually making life impossible or creating endless cases of diseases and deformities; (4) the inability to either solve the problems of the criminal or to rehabilitate the criminal, creating a society of locked doors, barbed wire, police dogs, and endemic fear; (5) the inability to stop the increase of the use of drugs, creating a large, unhealthy population of drug-addicted people and all the woes that go with such a situation; (6) the psychological trauma that an anticipated nuclear war causes, and the terrible unimaginable results if there were such a war; (7) the inability of the nations of the world to prevent population growth beyond the limits of the earth to sustain it and the mass starvation that will eventuate; (8) the potential threat (very real to some) that some form of biological experimentation will get out of control and will either destroy life on our planet or large populations thereof; (9) the resolute opinion of Freud (and such followers as Ernest Becker) that our neurotic problems are impossible to cure, and as a neutoric humanity we will ever compound our evils into larger and larger ones.[25]

From his own philosophical and theological perspective Huston Smith comes to a similar conclusion.[26] Whereas I have based my pessimism on the Christian doctrine of sin, Smith bases his on the takeover (at least in European-American territory) of scientism and evolution. He says the two options facing the West are: (1) embracing the great tradition found in all world religions and the history of Western philosophy (as documented according to Smith in Arthur O. Lovejoy's classic *The Great Chain of Being*) claiming that at center this is a universe of persons, of values, of morality, or meaning, and of purpose; or (2) accepting the current philosophy of scientism, which claims that the only real knowledge we have is that of the sciences. All else (such as those things Smith holds dear) are but bubbles (the philosophical word is epiphenomena) on the surface of the cosmos which—like all bubbles do—will eventually burst into nothingness.

In this context Smith introduces his views on progress. He is well read on this subject, referring to J. B. Bury, Karl Marx, Henri Bergson, Ernst Bloch, Jürgen Moltmann, Johannes Metz, and Pierre Teilhard.

If one asks if there is hope in progress in the long run—cosmic history!—the answer is no. The "heat death" of the universe means that eventually no life will be possible on this earth. If one asks if there is hope in the short run—say the next five hundred years—Huston's reply is identical to mine. The enormous destructive factors in our current situation make any hope for progress bleak.[27]

But modern humanity does hope, and we hope in progress. Smith is right when he says without hope we die. Hope does spring eternal in the human breast. The brainwashing of soldiers in the Korean war showed that if hope can be killed in a person's psyche that person (in this case a military prisoner of war) will literally, physiologically die.

However, Smith continues, this hope is no hope at all. It is first of all founded on *scientism*, namely, that our only valid knowledge is that given to us by modern science. One thing science cannot give us is hope, for hope is not in the vocabulary of science. Science may give us a more and more sophisticated civilization, but it cannot give us hope.

The real culprit in promising hope where there is none is *prevolution*. Smith coined this word by fusing together the words progress and evolution. Smith does not quarrel with science in its discussions of the cosmos in astronomy, or the current state of geological science, or the occurrence of fossils in the rocks. *Prevolution* means taking such data and illegitimately converting it into a grandiose evolutionary philosophy that explains all and gives modern humanity a sense of hope. Evolution in this sense is "the kingpin of the modern mind because from the standpoint of that mind so much has come to rest upon it—nothing less than hope itself—that modernity is more invested in this doctrine than in any other."[28]

Therefore, according to Smith, while no hope exists in science, there is some hope in the great tradition expressed religiously as a confession of reality as meaningful and expressed philosophically in the concept of the Great Chain of Being. I cannot but agree with Smith in general, although I differ from him in two respects. I believe sin is the deeper reason for not postulating inevitable progress; and my hope is more specifically the Christian hope.

VII

One of the assumptions behind the motto "art for art's sake" (*ars gratia artis*, l'art pour l'art) is that moral judgments have no place in art or that morality imposed on art corrupts it. This further implies that censorship in art (except of course in extreme cases) also corrupts or restricts art.[29] The early church fathers (e.g. Lactantius, Tertullian) as well as the later fathers (Augustine) were critics of the arts, especially the theater (and of course also the fights among animals, the fights of the gladiators, and the chariot races). The thesis behind such criticism is not merely that some works of art are offensive to Christian morality, but the more profound one that humanity as sinful can never be exempt in any territory from moral scrutiny. There is no territory of human activity that is automatically exempt from moral assessment, for every human activity is also by definition the activity of sinners.

Unfortunately the moral assessment of art is very difficult. Some Christian critics of art have a minimal understanding of the nature of art and its complexities and are boorish and amateurish in their judgments.[30] A work of art that may appear morally offensive at one level may be a profound commentary on human life at another level. For example, T. S. Eliot highly valued a novel (*Bubu of Montparnasse*) about the sordid lives of prostitutes in Paris because it was such an effective commentary on the Christian doctrine of depravity. A Christian making a moral assessment in the field of art may well appear a Philistine (one bereft of any appreciation of art and culture), a sterile moralist, or a graceless religionist.

The Christian position is that if humanity is sinful, then no human realm is sealed off from sin. The Christian therefore claims the right to the moral critique of all territories of human activity. Moral judgments are different from artistic standards. The moral critic of a novel does not presume to know more about the crafting of a novel than the author.

There is an unspoken Pelagian assumption that some professions have a humanizing and moralizing effect upon the members. The profession itself is assumed to have the power to lift the practitioner above the sordid level of human depravity. Christian theology challenges this unspoken assumption.

Physicians are bound by the Hippocratic oath, which is certainly one of the finest documents in the history of morality. Yet medical practice can be turned into sordid ambition, abuse of privilege, and in some cases criminal behavior. The lawyer follows an occupation whose supreme categories are justice and equity, yet many of the fraudulent schemes perpetrated on the public have been inspired by lawyers. It is estimated that one third of the cost of insurance policies is due to inflated costs from schemes concocted by lawyers. Politicians have a mandate to be guardians of the law, order, and welfare of the state, yet the sordid abuse of office is the common history of political life. Artists are creators of beauty, and it is difficult to think of beauty and sin at the same time. Yet artists have been conscripted to produce pornography for both magazines and films. People with literary gifts have written propaganda material for wicked states. Scientists are called to practice their skills with the purest motivations for truth and objectivity, yet their skills also have been used for destructive and immoral purposes.

To the Christian who knows the theology of sin none of this is new or shocking or unexpected. All people, before they are artists or scientists or lawyers are sinners. In the vivid language of Gen. 4:7 sin is like a demon crouching at the door of the sinner's psyche ready to spring into action with the smallest nod of encouragement. Nor is the Christian surprised when corruption is found in those agencies whose purpose is compassionate service of the wretched of the earth. Sleeping lions, like sleeping dogs, may be awakened at odd hours and in odd places.

VIII

In recent literature the word alienation occurs in many instances as a functional equivalent of the word sin. It was elevated to the role of a category of explanation by the German philosopher Georg Hegel (1770–1831). He used the term (*Selbstentfremdung, Entfremdung,* and others) to describe the tensions that emerge in the process of cultural evolution. Jean Jacques Rousseau first used the term in a sociological sense to describe bad relationships among groups. Karl Marx (1818–1883), who had read Rousseau, introduced the term into economics. In capitalism workers are alienated from the products they make because management takes it away from them for its own profit; and in turn the capitalist class and the laboring class are alienated from each other.

Since 1935 the concept has become more popular. It has the advantage in descriptive matters of being a morally neutral word compared to the word sin. In other situations alienation is used where in older literature it would be called the consequences of sin. Some existential philosophers use the word to describe the tension between essence (ideal existence) and that which a person actually is (existence). Used in this sense there is a core of alienation in each human being. In psychology it is used to describe a pathological situation in which one part of the psyche is out of touch with another part (this would not necessarily be sin but be a consequence of suffering from the imperfections of sin). Earlier in the century psychiatrists were called alienists! In sociology the word is applied to many situations that, again, historically would be called the effects of sin. One of the primary instances of alienation is the sense of loneliness and isolation people suffer when living in large urban centers. This was the theme of one of the more popular works on sociology in recent decades.[31]

Labor is alienated from management; parents are alienated from children and children from parents; husbands are alienated from wives and wives from husbands; pupils may feel alienated from the school system; young people feel alienated from the establishment; citizens feel alienated from bureaucratic government; voters feel alienated from the political process; elderly people feel alienated from the mainstream of community life; minority and racial groups feel alienated from the dominant community.[32] All of this historically would be called effects of sin but today is masked under the concept of alienation.

The industrial revolution, modern industrialization, and the growth of large cities were forces producing alienation. These forces have the net effect of breaking up traditional family and social groups and producing the lonely crowd. The relationships of persons to government agencies of all sorts, to social services, and to larger corporations becomes less and less personal and more and more bureaucratically impersonal. The great mobility of the population is a witness to the constant shifting of the business and economic world. This kind of transience also contributed to feelings of alienation.

Alienation means damage to the human psyche. Some call it existential lostness. Others call it *anomie*—the feeling of being in the midst of life with neither compass nor rudder. Others identify it as a feeling of helplessness as one feels the victim of pushes and pulls far beyond the limited power of the solitary person. Other symptoms of alienation are the increase in alcoholism and drug abuse. There is also some correlation of feelings of isolation with the abusive treatment of mates and children.

One can also find alienation in Holy Scripture. Cain murders his brother Abel from whom he is alienated. The alienated king Saul seeks to kill David. One of the indictments of sinners is that they are in a state of alienation from God.

Christian theology does have a special interest in the concept of alienation. It first of all is interested in the emergence of the concept as a category of significant interpretation in the nineteenth century. Further, the studies of alienation in the twentieth century, as well as the spread of the concept into many disciplines, is of help to the Christian theologian to understand in greater depth the phenomenon and its bearing on the Christian doctrine of sin. Certainly the concept of sin as a powerful force in creating endless forms of alienation is deeply embedded in Holy Scripture.

8. Sin Among the Theologians

There is no merit in rehearsing the history of the doctrine of sin another time. But there is merit in looking at some representative theologians in order to get a better perspective on the older versions of the doctrine and how more recent theologians have attempted to come to terms with them. A further purpose of reviewing some of these more representative theologians is to question if their version of sin enables them to see the human situation better, or whether a deficient view of sin also clouds one's vision of the human situation.

Friedrich Daniel Ernst Schleiermacher (1768–1834) is the founder of that theology known as liberal Christianity and is therefore an important theologian in an examination of the doctrine of sin.[1] Liberal Christianity did not reject the routine of Christian theology outright like so many Socinians and Deists, but it endeavored to retain the traditional theological topics while radically reinterpreting them. This is true of Schleiermacher.

Schleiermacher thought the essence of the Christian experience was a God-consciousness or a feeling of absolute dependence upon God. Schleiermacher attempted to reconstruct all of Christian theology, including the doctrine of sin, around that one affirmation.

As a theologian of liberal Christianity he rejected the historic Lutheran and Reformed doctrine of sin that included the Fall, Original Sin, and Total Depravity. He also rejected the definition of sin as breaking the law or deviating from an absolute moral code. He redefined sin as the interference with or the weakening of this God-consciousness. It is true that Schleiermacher cites the older creedal statements in fine print, but his interpreters consider this window dressing.

If sin is weakening the God-consciousness in a person then one can know what sin is only from the restoration of true God-consciousness. Redemption is all the processes that restore God-consciousness. In particular, it is the story of the God-consciousness of Jesus Christ and how that becomes gospel for us because it specifically grants us our true God-consciousness. Sin is then anything that inhibits redemption as understood in this sense.

That which inhibits or weakens our God-consciousness is our sensuousness or our flesh. Schleiermacher defines flesh as "the totality of the so-called lower powers of the soul."[2] It is the drag, the weakening, the inhibiting power of the sensuous part of our nature that then causes sin.

When a person is born into this world that person is already doubly penalized. First of all, the growing child experiences the sensuous before experiencing God-consciousness. The sensuous has the advantage in the sinner because of sheer priority in time. God-consciousness is a later adult experience and must work against the prior achievement of the sensuous. In a simple sentence, flesh precedes Spirit.

The second penalty is that the child comes into a world where sin has been established for a long, long time. Schleiermacher calls the priority of flesh to Spirit the germ of sin; the establishment of sin in the human race is his version of Original Sin. Schleiermacher speaks of stocks, new families, larger human masses, tribes, and peoples as the context in which babies are born and hence share in the commonality of their sins.[3] Historically the church has tied the transmission of sin into the fact that all humans derive from the same biological stock even though sin is not to be defined biologically. Schleiermacher breaks with that tradition and interprets the transmission of sin in terms of its social dimension among peoples.

Schleiermacher's version of sin is inadequate, first, because it reflects too academic or abstract an approach. His definition of sin is very theological and philosophical. The gory, brutal, violent, inhuman, perverse, and demonic acts of people do not fit into the theory. Sinners do things for the sheer hell of it or to release raging feelings of hostility or to express their sadism in cruelest of ways or to satiate a boundless narcissism. These actions were not out of sight of a man who spent forty years in the center of a large city, but he never saw the life of that city in such a perspective as to have it materially influence his doctrine of sin. His definition is too much that of a gentle, devout, godly pastor-preacher-theologian.

Schleiermacher's definition of sin has a second weakness. It is primarily a psychological definition of sin—that which hinders God-consciousness. That is the same kind of error ("categorical mistake") of attempting to define crime in psychological terms. Crimes are against specific laws of the city, county, or state. No doubt there are psychological elements to both crime and sin, but they are defined by an objective nonpsychological referent point. To define sin exhaustively in psychological terms is not to define sin at all—at least in the judgment of Karl Barth.[4]

III

We have reviewed Georg Hegel's (1770–1831) philosophical interpretation of sin. One aspect of it must be emphasized, as it strongly influenced the development of the theology of sin in liberal Christianity. In Hegel's thought sin was a necessary phase in human development. Humankind must cross the line from the innocence of the animal to the moral maturity of the human being. Adam and Eve had to eat the apple. Beasts may remain in innocence, but not human beings.

From this is derived the notion of the upward Fall. How can the Fall move in the wrong direction? It was a necessary step in the upward spiral of the human consciousness, so it was an upward Fall. It only appears to be a Fall, for the feelings of guilt and shame are not pleasant feelings. Many sins are very ugly, even brutal, but this is part of the price the race must pay as it ever spirals higher in its cultural evolution.

A further Heglian concept reflected in liberal Christianity is that the essence of sin is selfishness and that of a special type. Selfishness is a person's refusal to participate in the upward cultural spiral. To sin is to go one's own private way and ignore the cosmic process, especially as it is reflected in one's national culture. Hence in liberal Christianity sin is the selfishness of having no interest in the social goals of the kingdom of God. The religionist's faith is totally personal; and the secularist is indifferent to matters \ of the common good. Walter Rauschenbusch illustrated this point when defining sin in his last work, *A Theology for the Social Gospel*.[5] His major thesis is that sin is selfishness in its essence. And selfishness in turn is defined as refusing to take seriously, and practically into life, the social demands of the kingdom of God.

IV

Friedrich Schleiermacher transferred the notion of Original Sin from the biological unity of the human race to the social expansiveness and continuity of the human race. Sin was lodged deeply in society. Later in the nineteenth century Albrecht Ritschl (1822–1889) spoke of the kingdom of sin. With Schleiermacher, Ritschl denied the historic Lutheran and Reformed doctrines of Original Sin. In ethics Ritschl understood the kingdom of God to be the extension of Jesus' teaching of love to every dimension of human culture. As the kingdom of God spread it encountered the massive opposition of sinful people in society. Hence if there is a kingdom of God there is a kingdom of sin.

Ritschl's theory of the kingdom of sin was his version of Original Sin. The sinful state of society is not due to the Fall of the original pair but due to the momentum of sin in society itself. The kingdom of sin, which is so powerful, as a matter of course contaminates us all.[6]

Theologians like Ritschl and later the Social Gospelers advanced the theology of sin by going beyond the personal dimensions of sin to its social dimensions. Society itself can be sick with sin. Sin is not only the vices of persons but the way in which society is put together. Today the expression "sinful structures of society" is common. Hiring and promoting policies of a corporation may discriminate against minorities. Intelligence tests favor groups with certain cultural backgrounds. The list of such social manifestations of sin is long. In this perspective personal salvation is no panacea for social evils. The social structures themselves must be changed.

Although the Social Gospel existed prior to Walter Rauschenbusch (1861–1917), he is identified as its prophet. He gave much attention to the theology of sin in his last work, *A Theology for the Social Gospel*.[7]

Rauschenbusch returned as a young student to the Germany of his parents and attended a Gymnasium (a high-level college preparatory school). Later in life he again returned to Germany and learned the prevailing liberal theology of the time. All biographers of Rauschenbusch remark that he never forsook the deep Lutheran piety of his parents (although he was a Baptist) and never forsook the need of personal regeneration.

However, his experiences in a German Baptist church in Hell's Kitchen, New York, showed him the inadequacies of a ministry whose only goal was seeking people's personal salvation. The real problems were not the personal sins of the parishioners or the general population but the unjust way society was put together. Therefore what was needed was a social program, a Social Gospel, to eliminate the sinful structures of society and so relieve the evil pressures on the population.

A Theology for the Social Gospel is a transcript of popular lectures and not a piece of scholarly theological writing. Nevertheless, the ideas popularly expressed could be the foundations of a more academic book. In it Rauschenbusch shows no patience for the traditional doctrine of sin nor with the older theologians and older theologies that defended it. He accepts at face value the reigning critical opinions of the day about the book of Genesis and also states that evolutionary theory puts all in a new perspective. He admits great admiration for Schleiermacher and Ritschl especially in their notion that sin is to be understood in its social dimensions. As far as biblical materials are concerned, he places himself with Jesus and the prophets over against Paul.

Rauschenbusch of course believes that personal sin is wrong

and vile habits are not Christian. But he complains that when we define sin too personally and privately we mask the great social sins around us. It is not personal or private sins which do the real damage. The real evils done to humanity are committed by the larger sinful units—the kingdom of evil and the suprapersonal forces of evil. This might be the liquor industry or any corporation or factory which systematically suppresses and cheats the workers. It could be any oppressive government, and of course war is the worst culprit. Sinfulness is basically acts that are unsocial and antisocial.

Whatever may be salvaged of the older doctrines of the Fall, Original Sin, and Depravity is whatever value they have in helping us see the wide social dimensions of sin, the momentum of sinful practices once established in society, and the solid hold wicked people keep on their sinful control of institutions and other people. In harmony with many other theologies of liberal Christianity he thought much of our sinful activity was due to "evolutionary drag." We still carry with us from our animal behavior instincts that are at odds with our more refined civilized instincts.

However one assesses the Social Gospel movement it is generally recognized as the first in the history of theology to clearly articulate sin as manifested in social institutions and the way society is put together. The theology of sin must include the sinful way commerce may be carried on or corporations administered or social groups suppressed.

However, Rauschenbusch's thought is inadequate in at least three ways. (1) Some of his theological assumptions ought to be challenged, such as pitting Jesus and the prophets against Paul, or affirming that Jesus died for the kingdom of God. (2) The optimistic mood in his writings must be seen in the light of the eruption of realistic theology as a corrective to the optimism of the earlier defenders of the Social Gospel. Little did Rauschenbusch know that the demons were in the wings and would erupt in the 1930s. (3) Finally, the treatment suffers from an underestimation of violent personal depravity. Rauschenbusch was too preoccupied with the petty preaching about superficial sins in evangelistic sermons. Like Schleiermacher, Rauschenbusch does not take the full measure of sin by not noting the terribly depraved things human beings can do to one another.[8]

V

In discussing Søren Kierkegaard we noted that he pioneered an existential interpretation of Gen. 3. In Kierkegaard's thought Gen. 3 is not about a historical event but is rather the existential cross section of the act of sin. Therefore it is the diagnosis of every person's fall from God into sin. This version of the Fall by Kierkegaard has had a wide reception in the twentieth century. It is the resolution of the problems of Fall and Original Sin adopted by the Roman Catholic, Urs Baumann.[9] It is also the stance of Emil Brunner. In an existential context he defined his position as follows:

This then is the actual man, this being who lives in [existential] contradiction. Because man is in opposition to his divine origin in the Creation [essence], daily renewing this opposition, he lives in opposition to his own God-given nature; therefore his present nature itself is: contradiction.[10]

Certainly Reinhold Niebuhr and Karl Barth stand generally in this tradition. Niebuhr depended heavily on Kierkegaard and Brunner for his views of the Fall. Although Karl Barth does not set out an existential framework for his thought, his belief that Adam is the code word for all of humanity places him broadly in this tradition. And no doubt a much longer list could be made of theologians of the twentieth century who have been profoundly influenced by Kierkegaard in their theology of sin.

However the person who worked out Kierkegaard's insights in detail and precision was Paul Tillich.[11] Three observations are necessary to see Tillich in the proper perspective. First, to keep his theology in a relatively small manageable size he writes very concisely and compactly with virtually no documentation. Second, he writes from the perspective of an avowed existentialist. He wrote that "existentialism is the good luck of Christian theology" (p. 27).

The entire range of the topics of Christian theology are to be given an existential reinterpretation. Third, he writes his theology by staying with the traditional lists of theological topics and so addresses himself to the topics of the Fall and Original Sin.

Surprisingly for a theologian who greatly respects the Enlightenment, Tillich takes Gen. 3 very seriously but, as he emphatically affirms, not literally. In rejecting the literal interpretation he also rejects the historic church doctrines built on a literal interpretation and sides with the Enlightenment in rejecting the traditional interpretation. Understood mythologically and existentially Gen. 3 remains a great text on the doctrine of sin. Understanding Gen. 3 literally led Augustine and his followers astray.

Tillich begins with the distinction between essence (the model, the plan, the norm, the "God-intended") and existence (specific, concrete, individual human life). Only God is the perfect union of essence and existence. The rest of creation slips to some degree from essence into existence. People are born into this world according to a universal cosmic law; this involves some slippage from essence to existence. A human being lives in every moment of existence in that tension of the person's essence and the person's specific existence. This is the possibility of sinning.

In the next section of his development of a theology of sin Tillich depends heavily on Kierkegaard. He gives Gen. 3 an existential interpretation. Although all animals too slip from essence into existence (no dog is a perfect dog), only humanity has freedom and therefore consciously feels this slippage. Humanity in freedom and in the tension between existence and essence experiences existential anxiety. Tillich also postulates "dreaming innocency" as the state of a person in the anticipation of sin but not yet sinning. Further, Tillich constantly insists that these states do not take place serially in time (these are not steps with a before and after), but they are the constant and continuous factors in human existence. To these concepts he adds one more: the reality of temptation. The tendency to use one's freedom to pull away from dreaming innocency into a commitment to sin is temptation.

Temptation creates the state of alienation. The pull of concrete human existence away from essence is alienation, or estrangement, but it is not yet sin. Tillich is caught in a tight corner. If the estrangement of essence and existence were itself sin, then as a matter of fact there would be no sin. Estrangement is the predisposition for sin but not sin itself, so one cannot accuse Tillich of teaching that simply to be human is also by definition to be a sinner (although I am not sure he can evade this charge given the full range of his system).

One must give Tillich credit for refusing to give up the word sin. Estrangement or alienation are not synonyms for sin (p.46). The concept of sin must be retained in theology not only because it is the traditional word in historic theology, but more importantly because it emphasizes the personal decision in the act of sinning.

Sin, for Tillich, is thus personal decision responding to the alienation caused by the split between existence and essence. Tillich then offers a very rich discussion of the nature of sin from which (if one quietly ignores the existential backdrop) a great deal can be learned. Sin is *unbelief*, for in the act of sin the person turns away from God, the infinite ground of being, to something finite, "of this earth," having limited existential value. Sin is *hybris* or defiance, in which humanity decrees that its own wisdom is the royal road to fulfillment or happiness. *Hybris* underestimates human finitude, human weakness, human errors, human ignorance, human insecurity, human loneliness, and human anxiety. Sin is *concupiscence* in that sinners wish to draw all of reality into themselves. It is the unlimited human striving for knowledge, sex, and power. Sin is *act*. It is moving from the potential of sin (as described above) to the actual event of sinning. The possibility of sinning is a given in the universe; it becomes a reality only in the specific act. Sin is *demonic* in that there are forces and structures in society greater than any given person, creating evil in corporate human existence. Finally, sin is *collective* in that we not only sin privately but participate in the endemic and epidemic sins of our culture.

Tillich is aware of the charge that liberal theology held an unrealistic view of the sinfulness of the human race. He does not want to be caught in that superficiality. He writes after World War I,

World War II, the Hitler regime, and the Stalin atrocities. He wants to retain all the profoundity of the doctrine of sin as found in the Augustinian-Luther-Calvin tradition, but without its literalism regarding Gen. 3 and the rest of Scripture. He thinks that his existential version of sin avoids both the superficiality of the liberal doctrine of sin and the gross biblical literalism of the historic doctrine of sin.

Tillich's doctrine of sin is a rich one, but it is nonetheless limited. First, his existential presuppositions dominate the texts of Scripture. One does not find careful biblical exegesis in Tillich's theology, but rather interpretation by existential imagination. Second, Tillich gives the impression that there are only two ways of interpreting the biblical text (either literal-historical or existential). Recent literature on the subject shows that there are other valid options for the mode of interpreting these texts, such as Scharbert's concept of theology by narration. Third, in view of his Ground of All Being (which a number of interpreters take as veiled pantheism), is there really sin against God? If God is not the personal moral Judge, the standard of holiness and rectitude, the I AM of Moses, can sin be realistically understood? Perhaps in Tillich's theology, sin is reduced to existential error. Finally, Tillich does not believe in either immortality of the soul nor resurrection of the body. Eternal life is the *now* character of Christian life in this world. Death ends all. With the eternal perspective gone, we must ask if sinning or not sinning, being authentic or inauthentic, is all that important. If our life evaporates at death like the morning mist before the burning sun, is there any great moment about its moral quality?

VI

One of the most elaborate discussions of sin in the history of theology is that of Karl Barth. It confronts the expositor with great problems, because although the central discussion is contained within one volume,[14] expositions of sin are sprinkled throughout the *Church Dogmatics*. Furthermore, Barth worked most extensively on *Church Dogmatics*, IV/1, so it is jammed with all kinds of historical and exegetical details.

Barth's intention resembles that of Tillich and Berkhof. He wants to retain as much of the historic doctrine of the church as possible and yet expound a modern, relevant, and believable version. In Barth's theology Adam represents not an individual (although biblical texts may treat Adam that way) but the entire race of fallen people. Hence no Eden or Golden Age stands at the head of human history; when humanity appears, sin appears. Nor do humans inherit sin. Although not specifying Kierkegaard, Barth's view of Gen. 3 is essentially Kierkegaardian.

The most revolutionary aspect of Barth's doctrine of sin is where he locates it in his theology. Traditional texts discuss creation, then humanity, then the lapse into sin, followed by the doctrine of salvation through Christ. Barth, however, refuses to discuss sin apart from the doctrine of reconciliation. He believes we can understand sin only within the doctrine of the person and work of Jesus Christ. Therefore, he discusses a theology of sin within the volume treating the cross, resurrection, and the doctrine of justification. This volume (IV/1) is entitled, "The Doctrine of Reconciliation."

His arguments sound familiar. There are not two Gods—one acting outside of Jesus Christ who convicts us of sin and one in Jesus Christ who brings salvation. The one God and Father of our Lord Jesus Christ tells us *both* that we are sinners and that we have a Savior. Only through the person and work of Jesus Christ can we truly understand sin.

Barth admits that people may feel guilt or remorse or know they have offended God. But these are only the general feelings of human weakness and misery; they are not a knowledge of sin. We can really know what it means to be a sinner in the sight of God only by understanding all that Jesus Christ had to suffer on the cross.

In the traditional Roman Catholic and Protestant theology the plan of God works in three stages: (1) humanity is created in the state of righteousness or integrity; (2) humanity—in a datable event—disobeyed its Lord and Creator and fell into guilt and depravity; (3) Christ comes as God's dear Son to restore us back to fellowship.

Barth eliminates the first stage. His Adam is the Adam of 1 Cor. 15, the primordial human sinner. Barth opts for a strong Augustinian doctrine of sin without the Augustinian schema of (1) original righteousness, (2) fall and depravity, (3) rescue in Christ. Again, Barth eliminates the first step.

Barth affirms that the story of Adam is the story of each one of us. We are all Adam. Yet, as Adam, each of us is also the race. He wishes to keep the solidarity of the race in sin.

Although Barth's effort to take the full measure of sin is admirable, the traditional three-phase program outlined above seems truer to the biblical record than Barth's two-phase program.

VII

The Dutch theologian Hendrikus Berkhof has attempted to write a theology avoiding "rigid traditionalism" and "rudderless modernism."[13] His comments on sin reflect this effort (pp. 187–210).

His basic anthropological premise is that humanity is a creature characterized by freedom and summoned to live in love. Both human freedom and the summons to live in love presume the existence of a God who has spoken a Word, and the human ability to hear and respond to that Word. Therefore humanity is "the risk of God," for in freedom they may refuse or agree to live in love. The outcome is not predetermined.

Like Tillich, Berkhof wants to retain all the serious substance of the doctrine of sin—especially in his tradition of Dutch Calvinism—and yet not be caught in the limits of a very literal interpretation of Gen. 3 or a doctrinaire interpretation of Rom. 5:12–21. He wants to come to terms with Satan and the demonic and yet not in the literalistic sense of his forerunners in theology.

Berkhof's doctrine of sin clearly departs from earlier formulations. He denies the historic interpretation of Gen. 3; he denies the concept of hereditary sin as traditionally taught; he denies that Rom. 5:12–21 sets up a binding correlation of Adam and Christ, especially as found in federal theology; he denies the concept of an Eden followed by a historic, specific event called a Fall.

Basic to his treatment of sin is his definition of the human person. Humanity possesses freedom and finds beatitude in anchoring life in the holy love of God. Sin is the abuse of this freedom by refusing to ground oneself in God's love (p. 189). All else is commentary on this definition of sin. Gen. 3 is not about a historical event. Like Kierkegaard and Tillich, Berkhof sees it as a commentary on the structure of sin and the universal state of humanity. Gen. 3 is the story of every person's abuse of freedom and refusal to live in the holy love of God.

Berkhof does not want to get caught in some of the traditional traps. He denies that creation immediately implies sin. Creation and sin are two different categories. He wishes to avoid the dualism of Manichaeism and the superficialities of Pelagianism and religious liberalism. While retaining the notion of sin as pride (*superbia*) and concupiscence (*concupiscentia*), he wishes to avoid the turgid pessimism of Augustine's doctrine of sin.

Regarding the knowledge of sin, Berkhof asserts that one's definition of sin is related to one's system of values. All cultures have their lists of sins based on their systems of values. However, because of Jesus Christ Christians have the clearest knowledge of sin. The knowledge of sin in the cross is normative (the highest revelation) but it is not exclusive (people may rightfully feel sinful based on other criteria).

With reference to the origin of sin, Berkhof dismisses both dualism and the notion that God decreed sin for his own purposes and glory. He observes that we cannot avoid the ever-recurring notion that human freedom is the root of sin. It has been the only thesis to survive criticism. The origin of sin is in the "mysterious misuse of the freedom given [to humanity]" (p. 199).

Berkhof next plunges into the more profound aspects of sin, linking it to Satan, the tragic, and to fate. Essentially, he reduces the satanic to the tragic dimensions of sin. In the tradition of Schleiermacher, Ritschl, and Rauschenbusch he mentions the societal structures of sin. Sin is both *interpersonal* (the powerful effects sinners can have on each other) and *suprapersonal* (". . . the driving force inherent both in institutions of our established society and in the anonymous powers of current codes of behavior, taboos, traditions, or the dictates of fashion." p. 208).

A very brief evaluation of Berkhof's version of sin yields these observations. Berkhof claims that sin can be defined only in negative terms. This definition fails to come to terms—as we have said many times before—with the violence and brutality of sin, the willful initiative of ruthless behavior, the truly demonic element of sin, and the cold and cruel calculations that precede acts of sin. Only in the palest sense can sin be defined as a negative or negation.

The most fundamental question is whether a theology of concessions can be a truly Christian theology. No one in theology wants to be an obscurantistic fundamentalist (or whatever unlovely theology Berkhof means by "rigid traditionalism"). But giving away large chunks of historic theology because of science or biblical criticism or the mentality of the Enlightenment does not create a viable theology either. We have other options for coming to terms with modern learning than a continuous strategy of concessionism. Although Berkhof admires Barth and learned much from him, I feel Barth is more consistent in relating modern learning to theological methodology.

VIII

The literature of Latin America liberation theology presents a paradox. There is very little discussion of sin according to traditional handbooks, yet almost every volume of its literature is a tractate on sin. Many of its basic themes can be found in Walter Rauschenbusch's *A Theology for the Social Gospel*.

One common theme is that sin must not be privatized. This means that the concept of sin must not be limited to a discussion of personal sins or the seven deadly sins or the sins of the confessional. Rauschenbusch was right; there is such a thing as social sin. That which is doing such terrible damage to Latin American countries is sin in its social dimensions. The doctrine of sin must be politicized in the sense that it must move on from personal sins (not to omit them) to those structures in society that cause so much evil in the form of oppression, disease, hunger, and unemployment.

The central concept to describe sin in Latin American theology is oppression. Oppression is that which prevents our authentic humanity from developing and is therefore a crippling, shrinking, dehumanizing power. In the concept of oppression liberation theologies advance beyond Rauschenbusch. The common concept of oppression unites Latin American liberation theology with black theology, third world theology, and feminist theology.

Latin American theologian Orlando E. Costas[14] and other theologians in the tradition of liberation theology do not eliminate personal sin from consideration either. Their emphasis lies rather on those social sins causing so much grief in Latin America: imperialism, neocolonialism, exploitation, international cartels, dictatorial governments, landlessness of the masses, endemic unemployment, brutal dictatorships, hunger, and disease.[15]

The most controversial element in the Latin American theology of sin is its use of Marxism.[16] It claims to read Marx with open eyes, meaning it is apprehensive about items in Marx that are not compatible with Christianity. But it does claim that the Marxist analysis of society and its evils helps Latin American Christian theologians to diagnose their own situation.[17]

That conditions in Latin American countries are terrible is now public knowledge by virtue of television news reporting. By singling out oppression as the major category for a theology of sin, Latin American liberation theology has enabled us to see this kind of endemic sin. It has in every way expanded and enlarged the insights about social sin pioneered by the Social Gospelers. But it also presents certain theological difficulties.

Its theology of sin (as its Christology) is so overwhelmingly shaped by Latin American conditions that it is in serious danger of losing touch with the central Christian tradition. Christians live in a great variety of cultures (East German, Albanian, Russian, South

African, Chinese, etc.). If each of these Christian communities developed its own unique particularized versions of Christian theology it could potentially threaten the common theological heritage that binds us together. This is already a danger in Latin American Christology, where the theme of Christ the Liberator is difficult to harmonize with the established Christology of Nicea and Chalcedon.

The theology of sin of Latin American liberation theology needs to balance its accusing finger of a Nathan the prophet ("You are the [sinful] man," 2 Sam. 12:7), with the penitence of the publican ("God be merciful to me a sinner," Luke 18:13). Personal confession of sin and repentance is the first Christian virtue and the prerequisite for prophetic teaching.

The concept of sin in liberation theology must not play down the violent, demonic, brutal, and inhuman nature of personal sin. Multinational cartels may be exceedingly sinful in the results of their policies, but that should not mask our vision of the brutal husband, the psychopathic killer, the molester of children, or the murderer who kills by torture.

Finally the strategy of liberation theologians to use that part of Marx which helps their cause and exclude the other Marxian materials has been challenged. Wherever Marxism becomes dominant in a country, its proponents have been brutal and cruel to the Christian church and the Christians who come under their jurisdiction. To imagine in such situations that one can divide Marx into the good Marx and the bad Marx is unrealistic. Therefore, the theory of the liberation theologians that they can accept one part of Marx and deny the other part is a pure paper solution which could never work in the sordid realities of life.

9. The Rationale for the Doctrine of Sin

I

According to Blaise Pascal, without the Christian doctrine of sin one can understand nothing; with it one can understand everything. The test, then, of the Christian doctrine of sin is whether or not it has this illuminating power.

Rudolph Bultmann (1884–1976) claimed that the benefit of the Christian kerygma was that it granted the believer a new understanding of the self (*Selbstverständnis*). Even though he was thinking exclusively within the framework of existentialism, Bultmann made a significant point. If the Christian doctrine of sin does not clarify a person's own self-understanding it is not a meaningful doctrine. Some Christian doctrines have been historically important without clarifying personal existence (such as the *perichoresis* of the persons of the Trinity). But a doctrine of sin must clarify one's self-understanding, for it is a very serious pronouncement about the most personal dimensions of our existence.

Furthermore, the Christian doctrine of sin must help us understand the nature of humanity's social or corporate existence. It must not be a mere addition to our knowledge of society but along with self-understanding must be at the center of our understanding. Again, if it does not have this power of clarification, it wil be meaningless.

This does not mean that the Christian doctrine of sin replaces all other explanations or necessarily competes with all other explanations. Humanity as sinner may be ruled by greed for money (cf. 1 Tim. 6:10, NIV), but nonetheless the science of economics retains its inherent dignity as a human study. Persons may be criminals because fundamentally they are sinners, but that insight does not displace either the psychology of the criminal mind or the sociological study of crime. The Christian faith claims only that its doctrine of sin is a shaft of light on human existence, yield-

ing a profound insight without which much of what human beings do would remain obscure.

II

A new self-understanding (*Selbstverständnis*) means that a person prior to conversion does not really understand himself or herself. Such a person does not have the right categories, the right
grid, the right perspectives that truly frame a person for what he or
she is. But with the coming of the gospel, a person receives new
insight and now sees, knows, understands, grasps what sort of
creature a human being is.

The classical literature of Europe and America abounds with
characters whose lack of self-understanding leads to tragic consequences. The beautiful young girl who thinks the world is made
for her pleasure finds her life shattered by men without moral
character. The young man who thinks the real life is made up of an
endless round of pleasures finds himself a debt-ridden prisoner.
The miser who scrapes for every last penny finds himself isolated
from the true fellowship of other human beings. Such persons and
a thousand more in our literature have no self-understanding.

The Christian doctrine of sin claims to add a necessary element
to human self-understanding. It declares that every person is a
sinner and that without this knowledge each of us lacks a fundamental ingredient in our self-understanding. Knowing that we are
sinners means we can then understand our relationship to God
and God's kingdom. We can understand why humans do certain
things, from the milder trespasses to the actions of a very ruthless
criminal.

The Prodigal Son represents an excellent example of this. In the
far country the Prodigal came to himself (Luke 15:17). To come to
one's self is to repent; to repent is to see one's life in the perspective of its sinfulness. In the process of "coming to himself" he
achieved self-clarification. He really did not know himself when
he asked his father for his portion of the inheritance, nor did he
know himself when he wasted that inheritance. He only received

a true *Selbstverständnis* when he realized his sinfulness. He then formulated his homecoming speech: "Father I have sinned . . ." (v. 18).

Luke's Gospel also tells of two men who prayed in the temple. The one who prayed a very religious prayer had no self-understanding. Not knowing that in the spiritual sphere he was a sinner he could not help but pray a mistaken prayer. But the person who had a true self-understanding of himself in the spiritual realm prayed, "God, be merciful to me a sinner" (Luke 18:13).

We need not belabor biblical examples except to mention the case of Paul. When he was a young man with remarkable religious achievements (Phil. 3:2–6) he had no true understanding of his spiritual status before God. Upon his conversion he discovered he was a blasphemer and a murderer (cf. 1 Tim. 1:13) and therefore made a postconversion confession, "I am the foremost of sinners" (v. 15). Paul's case makes it clear that one can be exceedingly religious and not have the self-understanding that comes from a consciousness of sinfulness.

The second kind of clarification the doctrine of sin brings to our self-understanding is the realization that we are sinners in our "mission control center." Out of that elusive center of the psyche come the orders for action. Since we are sinners in the very command center of our beings, we issue sinful edicts. In one occasion we lie; in another we steal; in another we cheat; in another we may swear; in another we may abuse a person; and in still another we become envious and jealous. Sometimes we have the sinful impulse but no action follows; in other instances the impulse leads to action.

One can dismiss such things by saying that it is just human nature, or that it is just being human, or that nobody is perfect. But such vague observations clarify nothing. On the other hand, as soon as we understand ourselves as sinners then such impulses and such actions are immediately clarified. We do not only issue sinful impulses or commands from our "mission control center"; we are at that very center sinners, and therefore issue sinful commands.

Knowing that we are sinners also clarifies the experience of temptation. As sinners we experience temptation not only in the outer world of persons or things (an expensive car or a fine piece of fur), but we experience a fulcrum for temptation inside us. A person who is not a Christian may be profoundly puzzled and disturbed by some violent experience of temptation. Not knowing that he or she is a sinner, the person has no basis for clarifying the experience. But those of us who know the doctrine of sin understand the structure of temptation. We too may have very profound temptations. The agony of the temptations of our sinless Lord is known to any reader of the Gospels. But even though the temptation may be exceptionally severe (such as being sexually enticed), through our knowledge of the doctrine of sin we at least know why we are so tempted.

Knowing that we are sinners enables us to understand the influence of other people upon us. The Scriptures are rich in examples of how persons cause other persons to sin. It explicitly says that a person is not to be influenced by a mob to do evil (Exod. 23:2).

The Christian who properly understands the Christian doctrine of sin knows that our own sinfulness and the manner in which it exists within us can create in us profound spiritual confusion. Knowing the doctrine of sin does not mean that we have a neat, simple map that guides us through treacherous territory. The existence of sin in the "mission control center" can cause chaos right in that center. This is the theme of Rom. 7. The great apostle himself, caught in this profound inward turmoil writes, "I do not understand my own actions" (v. 15). As paradoxical as it may seem, that is an utterance of great illumination, clarification, and self-understanding. Sin is in the very center of the psyche, and sin as a powerful force does produce that kind of spiritual confusion. Persons who have no understanding of the Christian doctrine of sin, or Christians uninstructed from Rom. 7, may go through experiences that can leave them bewildered and thoroughly drained.

We must not claim too much. An understanding of the Christian doctrine of sin does not clarify all, as Rom. 7 itself teaches. The human psyche with its great brain (at least ten billion active cells!), its great storehouse of memory, and its convolutions upon convolutions will not yield its whole range of secrets to any schema. We only affirm that the Christian doctrine of sin gives us a self-understanding without which we do not truly know ourselves. Pascal was right.

III

One territory from which the word sin has been vigorously excluded is that of psychotherapy. One of the standard symptoms of common neuroses is guilt. This guilt is called "unearned guilt" because it is not the product of wrongdoing but of a neurotic response to life. Any talk of sin aggravates the feelings of guilt. Further, the therapist is supposed to be a completely accepting and nonjudgmental person, so any talk of sin would interfere with therapy.

If sin is a basic category for the understanding of persons according to Christian theology, then it cannot be excluded from psychiatry or psychotherapy without cutting off one important insight into mental disorders. A fundamental question in philosophy is, "Why is there something and not nothing?" Paraphrased it would read: "Why are there mental disorders at all?" What is the ultimate presupposition of mental disorders or neuroses or psychoses? The Christian answer is that the human person is a fundamentally disordered person. Not all share the same measure of disorder, but every psyche is to some degree a disordered psyche. We are not attempting to explain why a given person is neurotic or psychotic but how neurosis and psychosis are possibilities for human beings.

Søren Kierkegaard pioneered this kind of diagnosis of the human psyche. He developed the concept of anxiety as the existential anxiety about the totality of life. The problem of the sinner is not this or that failing. Rather it is that the whole psyche is like a ship whose rudder is fixed at a wrong angle or like an airplane whose wing adjustments are permanently set askew. It is not that some personal sin causes neurosis; rather, the state of sinfulness makes mental problems possible. Kierkegaard focused his comments on every human being, not particular mental cases. The existential anxiety about life created by our essential sinfulness has a twisting and deforming power. The measure of the twisting and deforming is different in each person. Christians are not better informed than members of the counseling community, but to them the ultimate source of our mental disorders is not a mystery. In the imagery of Pascal, every sinner is like a king who has been deposed from his throne. Our misery is that we are fallen from the sublimity of the image of God. Otherwise we would not suffer the basic anxiety of life.

Popular opinion held by very fundamentalist people claims that mental disorders are due to sin in a person's life; if the sin is not obvious the disorder is imputed to hidden sin. Psychotherapists are quick and energetic in repudiating such a simple moralistic interpretation of mental illness. But a small trickle of psychotherapists believe this has gone too far. One of the more shocking books of the recent past is Karl Menninger's book, *Whatever Became of Sin?* Not only did he attempt to restore sin as a viable category for explaining both personal matters and matters of national life, but he also wanted to reintroduce it into psychotherapy. In this connection he wrote:

> I believe there is "sin" which is expressed in ways which cannot be subsumed under verbal artifacts such as "crime," "disease," "delinquency," "deviancy." There *is* immorality; there *is* unethical behavior; there *is* wrongdoing. And I hope to show that there is usefulness in retaining the concept, and indeed the SIN, which now shows some sign of returning to public acceptance. I would like to help this trend along.[1]

Also shocking in the area of psychiatry was O. Hobart Mowrer's book, *The Crisis in Psychiatry and Religion*. Mowrer titled the third chapter, "Some Constructive Features of the Concept of Sin," and the fourth chapter, "Sin, the Lesser of Two Evils." One of his strongest sentences is: *"Just so long as we deny the reality of sin, we cut ourselves off, it seems, from the possibility of radical redemption (recovery)."*[2]

In line with Menninger and Mowrer is M. Scott Peck's book *People of the Lie: The Hope for Healing Human Evil*. Peck's experience in counseling led him to the conclusion that some of his patients were not only neurotic but also evil. (If we substitute the word "sin" for "evil" in his book, most of the passages would undergo no significant change in meaning.) He calls these patients "people of the lie," because they are chronic, systematic, deceitful, and hypocritical liars in the counseling situation. They arouse both disgust and indignation in Peck and he believes rightly so. Such people are not only neurotics; they are also sinners.

We think that Menninger, Mowrer, and Peck are at the very edges of the therapeutic community in attempting to add sin or evil to the vocabulary of diagnosis. The words "sin" and "evil" will not start staring at us from the pages of books on counseling. Yet some evidence supports the Christian stance that there is no full self-understanding if we omit the category of sin.

IV

It may seem odd to ask if the category of sin has any illuminating power for the area of literature. Of course, at the most obvious and superficial level the concept of sin illuminates why salacious, trashy, and horrifying novels are written. It is but another way that sinners pander on sinners.

Sin and literature are related on deeper levels. The classic murder or detective stories and the classic westerns are the only pure morality stories left. They carry the message, be sure your sins will find you out. Agatha Christie was influenced as a child by a nanny who belonged to the small fundamentalist Plymouth Brethren group. As a result she felt all of her novels had moral overtones. First, the murderers of her books are always common, ordinary people, for murder is not the specialty of a few of the race but as sinners it is a potential for all of us. Second, the moral rule of the universe dictated that the murderer always be caught.

Great literature deals with conflict and tragedy. It ponders the conflicts and tragedies that sin introduces into human life.

The great poet, dramatist, and literary critic, T. S. Eliot (1888–1965), believed that the story of human history was the story of the great conflict of good and evil. This meant that a person could not be a great literary artist without believing this and attempting to work it into his or her art.

Any drama that we see (film or television or stage), or any novel that we may read will have significant appeal only if it contains genuine conflict; and the very fact of the conflict is a commentary of the fracturing power of sin in human life. And so the theology of sin illuminates literature at its heart.

V

To ask if sin illuminates philosophy is to enter a most thorny thicket. Especially in the twentieth century, some philosophers have narrowed down the proper territory of philosophy to such a specialized strip that questions about evil and morality are excluded. It could be a proper question to ask if this narrowing down of philosophy to almost a trivial function is itself not a sinful limitation. If the major role of philosophy is to clarify the meaning of life, or to clarify the nature of human existence, or literally to seek out the wisdom of life, then if it leaves out a most significant factor of human life it has failed its mission. From the Christian perspective, if it avoids a discussion of sin it has cut short part of the scope of clarification.

Sin should be most properly introduced in the subject of ethics (and certainly under the discussion of the problem of evil). However, most texts on ethics are preoccupied with defining the basic ethical principle. One would never guess from texts on ethics the unspeakable, brutal, and depraved things which humans commit every day.[3]

However, such existentialist philosophers as Martin Heidegger (1891–1976) and Jean-Paul Sartre (1905–1984) do manage to talk about sin, but not in Christian terms. Martin Heidegger discusses inauthentic existence. By this he means all those things we do while holding back our authentic selves. The act of gossip is speaking inauthentically. Writing a pot-boiler for money produces scribbling. When we are interested in events only for the sake of curiosity we react inauthentically. When we retreat from the hard decisions of life and go along with the crowd we act inauthentically. Heidegger does not use the word sin, but that is what these failures amount to. In addition, theologians influenced by Heidegger discuss the problem of sin. It must be important if, as many think, the most creative philosopher of the twentieth century includes sin as a central part of his philosophy even though he masks it as a neutral description of human existence.

Jean-Paul Sartre's special phrase for sin is bad faith (*mauvais foi*—or, sick faith). Bad faith is sin existentially understood. It contains an element of self-deception. It pretends to authentically come to terms with existence, but at heart it fakes it. Sartre's example is the young woman who flirts with men, may even pet with them, but never goes to bed with them, and still imagines she has expressed her full sexuality.

In patriotism or love or friendship or vocation, we either authentically give ourselves to it with no pretense; or else in deception we never make the full commitment and are guilty of *mauvais foi*—or in theological language, sin. The second great existentialist of the century has his own version of sin. Of course as the dedicated atheist that he was, Sartre would never use the word, but we must also observe that his entire life was full of intense moral indignation at so much of the passing scene.

Whenever philosophers turn to the full explication of human life they then must discuss sin even though it will be called something else. Further, philosophers who eliminate from their work the problem of human existence and do nothing to clarify it, leave a large gap in their philosophical perspective. They leave us mystified, wondering how they can observe the world's tragedies as daily witnessed in newspaper and television news without having it affect their philosophy.

VI

Scientific research and scientific theorizing are Pelagian in principle. They presuppose that if experimentation is carried on under very strict rules and theories are formulated with utmost rational care, scientists will arrive at the truth. Science allows for no cosmic demon (which René Descartes [1596–1650] postulated to universally deceive us), nor fallen sinful humans who prefer deceit or error to truth. The great Dutch theologian, Abraham Kuyper, did not feel that science should be exempted from scrutiny with regard to sin. He therefore gave some careful attention to the impact of sin on science.[4] His basic premise is that if a person is by definition a sinner, then sin will have some impact on whatever that person does. Scientists are sinners before they are scientists, and therefore the possible impact of sin on the scientific activity must be assessed. Kuyper divides his discussion in four parts: the effect of sin on the mind; the effect of sin on our motives; the effect of sin on our natures; and the effect of sin on our knowledge of God.

Most of Kuyper's discussion can be popularly summed up by saying scientists are human too; they make all kinds of mistakes and are subject to the same kind of temptations and pressures as the rest of the population. Kuyper is different in that he wants to trace the foibles, failings, prejudices, and mistakes to sin as their ultimate origin.[5]

Kuyper's detailed examination of the impact of sin on science (or scientists) can be summarized as follows. Scientists use their entire psyche (imagination as well as reason) in doing scientific work. The Christian doctrine of sin teaches that sin reaches every part of the psyche. Therefore, we may expect to discover its manifestations in the entire scope of the scientific enterprise. Kuyper offers no substitute for science, but he does offer the cautionary advice that nothing in science exempts it from the impact of sin. As a founder of a university and as the architect of Holland's educational system, Kuyper had a high regard for science. He felt that the scientific community as such would exert a check upon its members, which would minimize the impact of sin on scientific work. And certainly the ability to repeat experiments would not only weed out the subjective factor in scientific theories but would also act as a check of the influence of sin on science.

In discussing Stephan L. Chorover's book *From Genesis to Genocide*, we noted how gross sins could be found among the scientists. Such a list of gross sins can be expanded beyond Chorover's list. Scientists may have unholy passions for fame. Scientists may engage in unholy competition. In reviewing the sociobiology debate precipitated by Edward O. Wilson we saw how bitter and vitriolic exchanges among members of the scientific community may be. Another aspect of the shadow of sin over science is the matter of government grants to science departments of universities; and how the budgets of science departments live or die based upon the amount of government money received. Another darker shadow of sin is fraudulent experimentation or faking of the evidence.

At the secondary level of sin and science is the amount of cheating that goes on in classes in science. Students too are sinners before they are science students. And there is also much sinning connected with the competition to gain entrance into graduate schools or professional schools.

Having taught for more than four decades in Europe and Asia as well as the four quarters of America, I know in how many ways sin finds its way into academia. We are concentrating our remarks of sin in academia on science because science is the model for pure objectivity and impeccable ethical procedures. It is also the model for the reign of truth over all prejudices and biases. It is supposedly international and intercultural. The fact that sin may penetrate academia at its strongest point is a commentary on the power of sin.

All of this comes as no surprise to those who know the Christian doctrine of sin. This is not meant to put down science as an activity, scientists, or the students in science classes. It simply underscores Pascal's point that if one thinks from the perspective of the Christian doctrine of sin, then it is no surprise to find sin manifested in science and academia.

The third level of an analysis of sin and science concerns applied science or technology. The pollution of our skies, our air, and our water by the byproducts of technology is one of the major problems of the planet, and unless solved it could greatly diminish the life forms on the earth. And at the present time we have nuclear weapons and delivery systems capable of killing the world's population many times over.

If it is the function and the virtue of the Christian doctrine of sin to grant an adequate understanding of self and the nature of human existence, it certainly does so in the territory of science.

VII

If the Christian doctrine of sin illuminates human existence, it can shed light on the understandings of world religions. The Christian concept of sin is not one of those annoying concepts that is limited to the Christian community. Sin more widely understood as the sum of all those forces that destroy personal life, social life, and international relations is a concept as long as history and as wide as the human race. In this comprehensive sense it is a fundamental category for the study of world religions. The encyclopedist James Hastings's famous *Encyclopedia of Religion and Ethics* includes extensive articles on both sin and the Fall.[6]

All religions are religions of salvation. All religions postulate something radically wrong with human existence. In this sense they each have a doctrine of sin and they each have a way of salvation.[7]

VIII

The theology of sin illuminates politics in a number of ways. The first is in the inability of philosophers or political scientists to develop the best possible theory of government. Something clouds our vision in this problem so that we are confronted with radically opposite choices. The Greek pioneers in political theory, Plato and Aristotle, held different theories. Plato opposed democracy, as it was to him the tyranny of the mob, while Aristotle classified government by the tyrant as the worst possible form. Today the world is split among various democratic, socialist, and dictatorial states.

A second insight the theology of sin gives us in politics concerns the continued restlessness within any state. Granted, not all is due to sin. There are honest differences and genuine problems. But states are centers of all kinds of powers, privileges, authorities, perks, and financial gains. Lord Acton (1834–1902), one of the most prominent men in nineteenth-century English politics, is reported to have said "power tends to corrupt; absolute power corrupts absolutely." In that so much power resides in political office, there is also in political office the maximum temptation for the abuse of power. The sinful dimension of human nature plays a central role for the scrambles for power in any governing body.

Furthermore, a commentary on the power and prevalence of sin is that every state must have its army, police force, judges, courts, and penitentiaries. It is simply a brute fact of sociology that with the increase of population and urbanization comes the spontaneous increase of crimes.

The effect of sin on the body politic may be seen also in the governing bodies of towns, cities, counties, and of the nation meeting regularly around the calendar year to enact new legislation. Much of it regulates new developments in technology, business, industry, and transportation. But a significant part of it tries to regulate or curtail new ways—to use theological language—of sinning. There are always new faces, new methods, new versions to old schemes. New schemes arise from the new technology. Sinners think of unending ways to con the public, and legislative bodies must write unending laws to curtail them. All of this is painfully transparent from the perspective of the Christian doctrine of sin.

Treatises on political theory will not begin using the word sin. The sinfulness of the species is the repressed premise of the political process. Political theory is foreshortened if the concept is not at least in the shadows. Much is clarified if we presume entrepreneurs are sinners; politicians are sinners; business people are sinners; customers are sinners; con men are sinners; and the population is made up of sinners.

IX

Sociologists are as adamant as any group of scholars in resisting the use of the category of sin. The positivistic mentality rules there too, in that events, deeds, mores, customs, and family patterns are considered simply neutral phenomena. No doubt a number of topics occupying sociologists are social phenomena or statistical tables that are neutral as far as any moral evaluation is concerned. However, from the standpoint of the Christian doctrine of sin, sociology is overloaded with traditional problems that used to be called sins. Sociologists are concerned with divorce, child abuse, spouse abuse, crimes of all kinds, alcoholism, deviant sexual behavior, and so forth. For scholarly reasons theological categories are avoided as much as the language will allow. Crime is deviant or antisocial behavior. Immorality is now called being sexually active. Deviant sexual behavior is now called alternative sexual preferences.

Perhaps it would be wrong for textbooks in sociology to read like a text in theology or ethics. Of course the last thing that should occur in such a text is a sermon or definition of a normative standard. If sociology is a social science then it too must have the ethical and value neutrality of other sciences. But the person versed in Christian theology is not put off by the use of totally objective or value-free language found in sociology texts. Sciences have to develop a vocabulary fitting to them. But Christians claim that a doctrine of sin gives them some insights into sociological phenomena denied the purely secular sociologist. The human person is a sinner before he or she is a political animal—to use Aristotle's phrase. Although the Christian cannot anticipate all the forms sinning may take, or may not have the slightest idea of statistical rates, the Christian knows that every society will continuously bubble up (like the famous La Brea tar pits) sins both old and new. The surprise is in the new forms that sinfulness can express itself, but not in the fact that new modes of sinning are always with us. The vast landscape of human activity surveyed by sociologists rather clearly appears to Christian theology as an endless commentary on human depravity.[8]

X

The doctrine of sin also illuminates the science of economics, but, as in politics, it is the suppressed category. In fact, the literature of economics is filled with moral judgments, and moral judgments cannot be made without—again in theological language—the implication of sin. A Marxist ideologist says many harsh things about capitalism, painting it as the supreme evil in economics. Paradoxically, the Soviet paper *Pravda* voices stern moralistic judgments, while the official atheistic philosophy of Marxism places supreme confidence in science, which in principle is morally mute. Atheism cannot avoid planting a rather firm foot in the territory of sin. Rightist capitalistic literature identifies the big spenders as the big sinners. The moralistic rhetoric is without end in economics. Munitions manufacturers are the merchants of death. Advertising is professional misrepresentation. International trade is neocolonialism. The first world sinfully exploits the third world.

Part of the judgement assessed against Adam was economic hardship (Gen. 3:17–19). And economic hardship is truly hardship. Endless trafficking in vice is justified on the basis that it prevents starvation. Economic hardship creates an endless array of human miseries, frustrations, poor health, and premature death. Marx may have been correct in his point—echoes of Gen. 3:17–19—that the root of many of our major problems could well be economics.

The Christian takes no pleasure in indicating that sin richochets into the territory of economics and that economic problems generate misery. Liberation theologians in particular have shown how much the Holy Scripture itself is concerned with the economically oppressed—the widow, the poor, the orphan, the sojourner, and the alien. The point is simply Pascal's: the Christian doctrine of sin sheds extra light on every human activity.

XI

The Christian doctrine of sin is especially capable of illuminating certain aspects of sinful human behavior. First a word must be said of the character of the biblical revelation. Holy Scripture is a book of great variation and diversity. Handbooks and textbooks of theology are usually nicely organized and outlined. Such books give the impression that they are simply transcriptions of the sacred text. The opposite is the case. Holy Scripture more closely resembles a vast art gallery like the Louvre in Paris or El Prado in Madrid or the British Museum in London. Imagine an assignment in which a person was to spend a year wandering among the exhibits and then writing an essay on humanity. So the Christian doctrine of sin is more like distilling one's impressions from an extensive gallery than making a narrow transcript of biblical texts.

1. The first phenomenon is the brutal acts human beings do to each other, the so-called "man's inhumanity to man." This is most transparent in the reality of torture. When we think we have heard absolutely the worst in human torture, we learn of an even worse one. There is a profound reason why Gen. 4 is preoccupied with two murders. When the human heart wills to deviate from its Lord and Creator it may, can, and has lost the maximum respect for its colleagues created in the image of God. Murder is the final solution, for it is the total elimination of the problem. If sin is the maximum deviation from the Lord and Creator it will express itself in the maximum disrespect of the highest creation—male and female in the image of God. Torture is but the more sadistic manifestation of the will to murder.

Amnesty International released a 263-page document, *Torture in the Eighties,* which stuns the mind when we imagine how civilized we think the world is or ought to be.[9] The report revealed that torture is state policy in forty-nine countries of the world. Among the forms of torture mentioned are: starvation; electrical shock; electrical shock to the genital organs; suspension by arms; isolation without light, air, or medical attention; slapping both ears simultaneously; submersion in water to the point of suffocation; sexual abuse; chemicals that cause mental disorientation; mock executions; sulfuric acid burning of the skin; cigarette burns; plucking out fingernails; being hung upside down; blinding; amputation; and the usual run of brutality and floggings. One cannot explain this list on the basis that the human species is returning to animal behavior, for animals never do such things. It is consonant with the scriptural verdict that when people will to deviate from their Lord and Creator (Gen. 3) they may turn upon their fellow creatures, murder a brother (Gen. 4, Cain), and even come to the point of delighting in murder for hardly a sufficient reason (Gen. 4, Lamech).

2. The second phenomenon deals with the infinite subtleties of sin. The other side of the coin of the brutal grossness of sin in torture and murder are the most refined and subtle ways of sinning. A person may sin against others in conversation by choice of word or phrases or intonation of voice. Sin may appear in the form of shaded attitudes in personal relationships. Or clever or shrewd ways of behavior may sinfully harm other people.

All efforts to make a chart of sin into lesser or greater evils fail. Gross and brutal sin seems to be the worst; but one cleverly worded statement, one slight failure to act or report, may have far more terrible consequences than a brutal sin committed in a moment of great anger.[10]

3. The third phenomenon illuminated by the Christian doctrine of sin is the discovery of gross sin in Christian organizations, churches, and denominations. The notion that religious organizations somehow sanctify their officials or persons in places of responsibility is not at all supported by Holy Scripture. Some of the strongest language of condemnation in both the Old and New Testaments is directed towards the sins of persons in the very center of the religious cult. The obvious examples were Ananias and Sapphira (Acts 5:1–11). Participation at the very center of a godly organization has no special sanctifying effect, because before persons are members of such inner circles they are first of all sinners. Whether the sin is gross immorality or financial fraud, it should not come as a surprise even though it may well have the right to come as a shock.

4. The fourth phenomenon is that of spiritual indifference or sloth. Blaise Pascal wrote that so much of sin is spiritual indifference. A hunter may be more disturbed by missing a shot to kill a rabbit than by the issue of personal immortality. Gamblers may be more upset over losing a game than about the biggest gamble of

all, their own spiritual destiny. In more prosaic language, sin has the effect of making thick and calloused the spiritual sensitivities of the human person. Thus, as Pascal observed, at the point of people's greatest moment, their personal relationship to God and Jesus Christ, they are criminally indifferent.

The theologian who has written most extensively on this theme is Karl Barth.[11] He frames human sloth in a Christological context. Sinners discover sin as sloth only as they become Christian and can contrast their pre-Christian attitude with the total self-giving of Jesus Christ. So seen, sin is evil inaction, a persisting in a low level of self-enclosed existence, being the victim of one's own stupidity, and spiritual tardiness in failure to come to terms with the gospel.

5. Finally, a doctrine of sin illuminates the infinite capacity of the mind of the sinner to rationalize any sinful act or criminal practice or inhuman barbarism. The major tradition in Christian theology has affirmed that pride in the sense of the human defiance of God is at the center of sin. Others have suggested that the loss or lack of love is the worst manifestation of sin. There are some good reasons to think that sin at its worst is the sinner's endless ways of rationalizing his or her sin.

M. Scott Peck in his book *People of the Lie* deals with the process of rationalizing (attempting to give good and valid reasons for other than good or valid action). People of the lie are especially skilled in their boundless capacity to rationalize and so prevent even the beginning scratch of some helpful counseling. They are so wicked in doing this Peck thinks they are not only neurotic but evil.

Perhaps the most sinister form of sin as rationalization may be that demonic rationalizing that attempts to convert wicked acts, words, or practices into plausible good ones. In a modestly written but profound preface to his book, *The Great Divorce*,[12] C.S. Lewis writes precisely on this theme. He takes as his point of departure the title of William Blake's (1757–1827) work *The Marriage of Heaven and Hell*. Lewis remarks that the human race is ever attempting this marriage by attempting in moral terms, to turn evil into good. Evil can be undone (in acts of penitence, confession, forgiveness), but it can never be transmuted into good. If that can be done the whole moral ordering of the universe including humanity in particular is confounded. That rationalizing I have in mind, and the "people of the lie" that Peck has in mind are precisely attempting to turn evil into good. This is why the rationalizing of sinners about their sins might be the deepest infamy of all.

XII

In summary, our main thesis has been that of Blaise Pascal: (1) the Christian doctrine of sin is offensive to the reason and repelled by the intelligentsia and academia; (2) without this doctrine of sin much of human life and history remains forever opaque; (3) with it a shaft of light is cast upon personal existence, social existence, and the course of history, giving clarity that nothing else in the religions of the world nor the philosophies of the world can provide.

Our second thesis has been that the Christian doctrine of sin is not a provincial, limited, parochial Christian doctrine. All world religions have a theology of the misfortune of the human race. Their words for it differ from the Christian one, but the topic is common. Every great philosopher who has wrestled with the problem of evil has by implication wrestled with the problem of sin. Finally, if one wishes to list the actual and potential evils of our world from the small hamlet or African bush village to international relationships, one will be reciting those things in Christian language we would call either sin or the effects of sin.

Berkouwer ends his great book on sin with a chapter on "The End of Sin."[13] One might say that at this point begins the saving gospel of our Lord Jesus Christ and the final triumph of the Lamb of God as recorded in the book of Revelation.

Abbreviations

EB (15) *The New Encyclopaedia Britannica*, 30 vols. 15th ed. Chicago: The University of Chicago Press, 1975.

EP Paul Edwards, Editor, *The Encyclopedia of Philosophy*, 8 vols. New York: The Macmillan Company and The Free Press, 1967.

HERE James Hastings, editor, *Encyclopaedia of Religion and Ethics*, 13 vols. New York: Charles Scribner's Sons, 1928.

IDB George Arthur Buttrick, editor, *The Interpreter's Dictionary of the Bible*, 4 vols. New York: Abingdon Press, 1962.

IDBS *The Interpreter's Dictionary of the Bible: Supplementary Volume*, 1976.

ISBE James Orr, editor, *The International Standard Bible Encyclopaedia*, 5 vols. Grand Rapids: Wm. B. Eerdmans, 1939.

NIV *The Holy Bible:* New International Version.

SM Karl Rahner, editor, *Sacramentum Mundi: An Encyclopedia of Theology*, 6 vols. New York: Herder and Herder, 1968.

TDNT Gerhard Kittel and Gerhard Friedrich, editors, *Theological Dictionary of the New Testament*, 10 vols. Translated by Geoffrey W. Bromiley. Grand Rapids: Wm. B. Eerdmans, 1964–1976.

RSV *The Holy Bible*. Revised Standard Version

Notes

Chapter 1. The Question Posed

1. Blaise Pascal, *Pensées*, ed. Louis Lafuma, trans. A. J. Krailsheimer (New York: Penguin Books, 1966).
2. Ibid., p. 65, no. 131.
3. Ernst Cassirer, *The Philosophy of the Enlightenment*, trans. Fritz C. A. Koelln and James P. Pettegrove (Boston: Beacon Press, 1951), p. 142.
4. Philip H. Rhinelander, *Is Man Incomprehensible to Man?* (New York: W. H. Freeman, 1974).
5. This school of thought has come under very searching criticism by Alasdair MacIntyre in *After Virtue: A Study in Moral Theory* (Notre Dame, Ind.: University of Notre Dame Press, 1980).
6. M. Scott Peck, *The Road Less Traveled* (New York: Simon and Schuster, 1978), pp. 206, 207.
7. Julius Müller, *The Christian Doctrine of Sin*, 2 vols., trans. William Urwick (Edinburgh: T. and T. Clark, 1885), 2:268ff.
8. John Hick, *Evil and the God of Love*, rev. ed. (San Francisco: Harper & Row, 1966).
9. Andrew Fairbairn, *The Philosophy of the Christian Religion* (New York: Macmillan, 1902), pp. 132-68. For a more recent discussion see Alvin Plantinga, *God, Freedom, and Evil* (New York: Harper & Row, 1974), pp. 29-33.
10. Peck, *People of the Lie: The Hope for Healing Human Evil* (New York: Simon and Schuster, 1983), chap. 2, "Toward a Psychology of Evil," p. 36-84.
11. Quoted in *Eternity* 35 (April 1984): 15.

Chapter 2. If Adam Didn't, Who Did?

1. When the scholars and others renounced orthodox Christianity, they did not repudiate religion and become atheists. What they did do was to reject the supernatural element in Scripture and also the dogmatic content. Their new version of Christianity interpreted Christianity as essentially an ethical system. God was regulated to the status of an absentee landlord. This version of Christianity was designated as deism.
2. R. S. Peters, "Thomas Hobbes," *The Encyclopedia of Philosophy*, vol. IV (New York: Macmillan, 1967) pp. 30-46.
3. E. E. Kellett, "Spinoza," *Hastings Encyclopedia of Religion and Ethics*, vol. XI, pp. 768-784.
4. Voltaire, *Candide, Zadig and Selected Stories*, trans. Donald M. Frame (New York: New American Library, 1961).
5. Gottfried Leibniz's book *Essays on Theodicy and the Goodness of God, the Freedom of Man, and the Origin of Evil* (1710) defended the famous hypothesis that this current world is the best of all possible worlds. This view was in turn the center of attack in *Candide*.

6. Cf. the remarks by Ernest Becker on Rousseau in his work *Escape from Evil* (New York: Free Press, 1975), pp. 38-40.

7. Immanuel Kant, *The Critique of Practical Reason and Other Writings in Moral Philosophy*, ed. and trans. Lewis White Beck (Chicago: University of Chicago Press, 1949).

8. Kant, *Religion Within the Limits of Reason Alone*, trans. Theodore M. Greene and Hoyt H. Hudson (New York: Harper & Brothers, 1960).

9. Emil Brunner, *Man in Revolt: A Christian Anthropology*, trans. Olive Wyon (Philadelphia: Westminster Press, 1947), p. 126.

10. Mary Frances Thelen, *Man As Sinner in Contemporary American Realistic Theology* (New York: King's Crown Press, 1946), pp. 34-41.

11. We are again indebted to Thelen, *Man As Sinner*, pp. 41-53. Reginald Stewart Moxon in chap. 8 of *The Doctrine of Sin* (London: George Allen and Unwin, 1922) replaces the historical doctrine of the Fall and Original Sin with a psychoanalytic interpretation very dependent on Freud.

12. Becker, *Escape from evil*, p. 151.

13. I have treated Freud in more detail, pointing out some things Christians may learn from him, in *The Devil, Seven Wormwoods, and God* (Waco, Texas: Word Books, 1977), chap. 4.

14. B. F. Skinner, *Beyond Freedom and Dignity* (New York: Bantam Books, 1972).

15. Skinner has also presented his views in a literary Utopian style in *Walden Two* (New York: Macmillan, 1948).

16. Edward O. Wilson, *Sociobiology: The New Synthesis* (Cambridge: Harvard University Press, 1975). For the great ferment stirred up by the book and Edward Wilson's defense, see L. Caplan, ed., *The Sociobiology Debate* (New York: Harper & Row, 1978).

17. Vigorous (even at times brutal) criticism of Wilson may be found in Caplan, *Sociobiology Debate*, pp. 259-64, 280-90. Wilson's reply appears on pp. 265-68, 291-303.

18. Becker, *Escape from Evil*.

19. Stephan L. Chorover, *From Genesis to Genocide: The Meaning of Human Nature and the Power of Behavior Control* (Cambridge: MIT Press, 1979), p. 19.

20. C. S. Lewis, *That Hideous Strength: A Modern Fairy-tale for Grownups* (New York: Macmillan, 1946).

21. John Calvin's political theory is found in the famous last chapter of his *Institutes of the Christian Religion*, ed. John T. McNeill, trans. Ford Lewis Battles (Philadelphia: Westminster Press, 1960), bk 4, chap. 20. Calvin was concerned about the power play of the king or rulers and proposed as a check an old custom of both Greeks (the ephors) and Romans (tribunes of the people), whereby lesser magistrates in the state would be able to criticize the king or rulers without fear of reprisal (pa. 31). Karl Barth had similar apprehensions and approached a version of passive Christian anarchy, i.e., "all states are created equally evil." Cf. George Hunsinger, *Karl Barth and Radical Politics* (Philadelphia: Westminster Press, 1976).

22. Albert Camus, *The Fall*, trans. Justin O'Brien (New York: Alfred A. Knopf, 1957).

23. Camus, *The Plague*, trans. Stuart Gilbert (New York: Vintage Books, 1948).

24. I have treated *The Plague* in much greater detail in my book, *The Devil, Seven Wormwoods, and God* (Waco, Texas: Word Books, 1977), pp. 83-104.

25. Camus, *The Myth of Sisyphus*, trans. Justin O'Brien (New York: Vintage Books, 1959).
26. T. S. Eliot, *The Family Reunion* (New York: Harcourt, Brace, and World, 1937).

Chapter 3. The Case Against the Human Race

1. G. C. Berkouwer, *Sin*, trans. Philip C. Holtrop (Grand Rapids: Wm. B. Eerdmans, 1971), chap. 2, pp. 27-66.
2. We are deeply indebted to S. J. de Vries's masterful article in IDB, s.v. "Sin, Sinners."
3. Hans Walter Wolff, *Anthropology of the Old Testament*, trans. Margaret Kohl (Philadelphia: Fortress Press, 1974), pp. 40-58.
4. de Vries, "Sin, Sinners," p. 364.
5. Walter Bauer, *A Greek-English Lexicon of the New Testament*, translated and augmented by William F. Arndt and F. Wilbur Gingrich, 4th ed. (Chicago: University of Chicago Press, 1957, p. 877 (italics are his).
6. Cf. all the dilemmas that face such an expert commentator as C. E. B. Cranfield, *A Critical and Exegetical Commentary on the Epistle to the Romans*, 6th ed. entirely rewritten (Edinburgh: T. and T. Clark, 1975), 1:269-95.
7. H. Shelton Smith, *Changing Concepts of Original Sin: A Study in American Theology Since 1750* (New York: Charles Scribner's Sons, 1955).
8. Jonathan Edwards, *The Great Christian Doctrine of Original Sin Defended*, vol. 2 of *The Works of President Edwards* (New York: S. Converse, 1829), pp. 301-353.
9. Smith, *Changing Concepts*, chap. 9, pp. 198-230.
10. Søren Kierkegaard, *The Concept of Anxiety: A Simple Psychologically Orienting Deliberation on the Dogmatic Issue of Hereditary Sin*, ed. and trans. Reidar Thomte and Albert B. Anderson (Princeton: Princeton University Press, 1980).
11. Karl Barth, *Christ and Adam: Man and Humanity in Romans 5*, trans. T. A. Smail. Scottish Journal of Theology Occasional Papers, no. 5 (London and Edinburgh: T. and T. Clark, 1956).
12. Peter Lengsfeld has made a detailed study of Barth's views of Adam in which he reverses Adam-Christ to Christ-Adam and affirms that Barth's view is just the opposite of Paul's intention. *Adam und Christus: Die Adam-Christus Typologie im Neuen Testament und ihre dogmatische Verwendung bei M. J. Scheeben und K. Barth* (Essen: Ludgerus-Verlag Hubert Wingen, 1965), pp. 208-216.
13. H. Wheeler Robinson, *Corporate Personality in Ancient Israel*, rev. ed. (Philadelphia: Fortress Press, 1980). Gene M. Tucker wrote an introduction for the revised edition surveying criticisms of Robinson's concept, pp. 7-13.
14. James Orr, *The Christian View of God and the World as Centering in the Incarnation* (1893; reprint, Grand Rapids: Wm. B. Eerdmans, 1948).
15. Cf. Russell F. Aldwinckle, *Jesus—A Savior or the Savior? Religious Pluralism in a Christian Perspective* (Macon: Ga.: Mercer University Press, 1982); F. W. Dillistone, *The Christian Understanding of Atonement* (Philadelphia: Westminster Press, 1968). For the following survey see HERE, s.v. "Sin" (includes sections on all world religions); *Dictionary of the History of Ideas*, s.v. "Sin and Salvation"; *Shorter Encyclopedia of Islam*, s.v. "KHati'a"; *Encyclopaedia Judaica*, s.v. "Sin"; *The Universal Jewish Encyclopaedia*, s.v. "Original Sin."
16. Muhammad Hamidullah, ed., *Introduction to Islam*, 2d ed. (Paris: Centre Culturel Islamique, 1969). This is a very valuable book for Christians, as it very

clearly presents the Islamic faith in contrast to the Christian faith. Further, it is written in an apologetic spirit, sharpening the Christian-Muslim differences.

Chapter 4. If Adam Did, How?

1. Andrew D. White, *A History of the Warfare of Science with Theology in Christendom* (New York: D. Appleton, 1896), 1:256.
2. John C. Greene, *The Death of Adam: Evolution and Its Impact on Western Thought* (Ames, Iowa: Iowa State University Press, 1959).
3. Roman Catholic theology is involved in the Adam issue in *The Council of Orange* (529); *The Decrees of the Council of Trent* (1545-1563); and recently the encyclical *Humani Generis* of Pope Pius XII (1950). The Dutch Roman Catholic scholars in particular have written much attempting to correlate the New Adam with the traditional doctrine.
4. Lewis, "The Funeral of a Great Myth," *Christian Reflections* (Grand Rapids: Wm. B. Eerdmans, 1967), pp. 82–93; Huston Smith, *Beyond the Post-Modern Mind* (New York: Crossroad, 1982), pp. 169-74.
5. Paul Feyerabend, *Against Method: Outline of an Anarchistic Theory of Knowledge* (London: Verso, 1975).
6. We call attention to the cry of a very devout, orthodox Christian and professional geologist, J. R. van de Fliert, who attempted to establish the dignity and worth of geological science against prominent fundamentalist detractors. "Fundamentalism and Fundamentals of Geology: A Geologist's Response to Revived Diluvianism [so-called Flood Geology]," *International Reformed Bulletin*, nos. 32, 33 (1968), pp. 5-27.
   Attention must also be called to Michael T. Ghiselin's *The Triumph of the Darwinian Method* (Berkeley: University of California Press, 1969). Antievolutionary literature does not deal with the ideological and theoretical conflict of the pre-Darwinian scientists and the ideological and theoretical innovations of Darwin. Although Ghiselin writes with unbounded admiration of Darwin, he does tell us of this aspect of the dispute.
7. Bruce Vawter, *On Genesis: A New Reading* (Garden City, N.Y.: Doubleday, 1977), pp. 26-29.
8. Julius Gross has reviewed the history of the doctrine of Original Sin in *Entstehlungsgeschichte des Erbsündedogmas*, 4 vols. (Munich: Ernst Reinhardt, 1960-72). The fourth volume is given over almost entirely to Roman Catholic authors and their efforts to reinterpret the doctrine of Original Sin in the light of modern scientific knowledge.
9. Cf. E. A. Speiser, ed., *Genesis*, vol. 1, in *The Anchor Bible* (Garden City, N.Y.: Doubleday, 1964).
10. E.g., James Orr wrote, "I do not enter into the question of how we are to interpret the third chapter of Genesis,—whether as history or allegory or myth, or, most probably of all, as old tradition clothed in oriental allegorical dress,—but the truth embodied in that narrative, viz. the fall of man from an original state of purity, I take to be vital to the Christian view." *Christian View*, p. 185. W. H. Griffith Thomas, destined to be president of the Dallas Theological Seminary but prohibited by his premature death, wrote, "But if by myth is meant a form of picturesque teaching suited to the childhood of the world, it may be said that even if it be a myth in *form*, its underlying teaching and details must be true to

fact. Even parabolic teaching presupposes facts which correspond to the sym-
bol used." *Genesis: A Devotional Commentary* (Grand Rapids: Wm. B. Eerdmans,
1946), p. 25 (italics are his). Also such great literateurs and very orthodox An-
glicans as C. S. Lewis, T. S. Eliot, Charles Wiliams, and Dorothy Sayers had no
problem with the concept of myth, as they all viewed myth differently from the
radical biblical critics and the fundamentalists.

11. Josef Scharbert, *Prolegomena eines Alttestamentlers zur Erbsündenlehre*, vol. 37 in
Quaestiones Disputatae (Freiberg: Herder, 1968). The Jewish scholar Lou Hack-
ett Silberman says that the Jewish faith is built on narrative theology because
so much of Israel's reflective theological thought is embedded in Israel's history. EB (15), s.v. "Judaism," p. 284.

12. Approaching Gen. 1–3 from a different perspective but coming to similar conclusions is Henricus Renckens, *Israel's Concept of the Beginning: The Theology of
Genesis I–III*, trans. Charles Napier (New York: Herder and Herder, 1964).

13. G. W. Bromiley and T. F. Torrance, eds. and trans., *Church Dogmatics: Index Volume* (Edinburgh: T. and T. Clark, 1977), s.v. "Saga."

14. The case is reviewed in detail by John Timmer, "The Fall of Assen," *The Reformed Journal* 19 (October 1969): 15–20 and 19 (November 1969): 14–20.
Claus Westermann has written the most extensive commentary on Genesis in
the history of its exposition. He summarized some of his leading views in a
small book, *Creation*, trans. John J. Scullion (Philadelphia: Fortress Press,
1974), pp. 12–13. He thinks that the concept of myth has been abused by the
Bultmannian school. He claims it is wrong to oppose myth to history. However,
we prefer the terms narrative theology or theology by narration.

15. Cf. *Theological Dictionary of the Old Testament*, ed. Johannes Botterweck and
Helmer Ringgren, trans. John T. Willis (Grand Rapids: Wm. B. Eerdmans,
1974), s.v. "'ādhām."

16. Huston Smith, *Forgotten Truth: The Primordial Tradition* (New York: Harper &
Row, 1976).

17. Barth, *Church Dogmatics*, III/1. *The Doctrine of Creation*, trans. J. W. Edwards, O.
Bussey, and Harold Knight (Edinburgh: T. and T. Clark, 1958).

Chapter 5. The Center of the Theology of Sin

1. For a brief summary of these matters, see Heinrich Ott, ed., *Die Antwort des
Glaubens: Systematische Theologie in 50 Artikeln* (Berlin: Kreuz-Verlag, 1972), pp.
180–86.

2. Walter Rauschenbusch, *A Theology for the Social Gospel* (New York: Macmillan,
1918), pp. 59–61.

3. Kierkegaard, *Anxiety.*

4. Urs Baumann, *Erbsünde: Ihr traditionelles Verstandnis in der Krise heutiger Theologie* (Freiburg: Herder, 1970).

5. Gross, *Entwicklungsgeschichte des Erbsündedogmas seit der Reformation* (Munich:
Ernst Reinhardt Verlag, 1972), pp. 327–28.

6. Kurt-Heinz Weger, *Theologie der Erbsünde* (Freiburg: Herder, 1970), p. 75.

7. Cited by Weger, *Erbsünde*, p. 30.

8. Gottfried Quell, TDNT, s.v. "harmatano."

9. A sample of other theologians that could be classified in the generic tradition
are Paul Althaus, *Die christliche Wahrheit: Lehrbuch der Dogmatik*, 5th ed. (Gü-

tersloh: Carl Bertelsmann, 1959), p. 129; Wolfgang Trillhaas, *Dogmatik* (Berlin: Alfred Töpelmann, 1962), pp. 189–204.

10. Herman Bavinck, ISBE, s.v. "Fall," p. 1092.
11. Lewis, *The Problem of Pain* (New York: Macmillan, 1962), pp. 69–88.
12. Cf. Pascal, *Pensées*, no. 695. Norman Powell Williams granted that if there were not a historical human Fall there nevertheless must be a Fall. Hence he postulated the prehistoric cosmic Ultimate Fall. *The Ideas of the Fall and Original Sin: A Historical and Critical Study* (London: Longmans, Green, and Co., 1927). Lecture 8, pp. 489–530.
13. Cf. Westermann, *Creation*, pp. 17–31.
14. Helmut Thielicke, *How the World Began: Man in the First Chapters of the Bible*, trans. John W. Doberstein (Philadelphia: Muhlenberg Press, 1961), pp. 3–11, passim.
15. Heinrich Vogel, *Gott in Christo: Ein Erkenntnisgang durch die Grundprobleme der Dogmatik*, 2d ed. (Berlin: Lettner Verlag, 1952), pp. 469–512.
16. Stanton E. Samenow, *Inside the Criminal Mind* (New York: Times Books, 1984).
17. Vogel, *Gott in Christo*, pp. 469ff.

Chapter 6. Sin at Its Roots

1. Kierkegaard, *Anxiety*, p. 54.
2. Berkouwer, *Sin*, chap. 4, "Sin and the Demonic Realm."
3. Samenow, *Criminal Mind*, pp. 9–23.
4. O. Hobart Mowrer, *The Crisis in Psychiatry and Religion* (Princeton, N.J.: D. Van Nostrand, 1961), pp. 43–44.
5. Lewis, *The Great Divorce* (New York: Macmillan, 1946).
6. Henrich Seesemann, TDNT, s.v. "peria."
7. Thielicke, *How the World Began*.
8. Lewis, *Perelandra: A Novel* (New York: Macmillan, 1944). Fyodor Dostoyevsky's *Crime and Punishment*, trans. Constance Garnett (New York: Random House, 1960) could also be called a classic in the theology of temptation, for there are the strong temptations in the student, Raskolnikov, the rich goods of the lady pawnbroker, the conflict, the yielding to temptation, and the ultimate failure. Lewis is more theological in his approach; Dostoyevsky more psychological, even depth-psychological.
9. Karl Menninger, *Whatever Became of Sin?* (New York: Hawthorn Books, 1973).
10. Barth, *Church Dogmatics*, III/3, trans. G. W. Bromiley and R. J. Ehrlich (Edinburgh: T. and T. Clark, 1960), sec. 51, pp. 369ff.
11. Ibid., p. 369.
12. See IDB, s.v. "Demon," and W. O. E. Oesterly's article, "Demon, Demoniacs," *Dictionary of Christ and the Gospels*, 1:438–43, with its bibliography on non-Christian sources.
13. Friedrich Schleiermacher, *The Christian Faith*, translated from 2d Ger. ed. by H. R. Mackintosh and J. S. Stewart (Edinburgh: T. and T. Clark, 1928), 2d app., "The Devil," pp. 161ff.
14. John Livingston Nevius, *Demon Possession and Allied Themes*, 3d ed. (Chicago: Fleming H. Revell, 1895).
15. Peck. *People of the Lie*, chap. 5, "Of Possession and Exorcism."

16. Hendrikus Berkof, *Christian Faith*, trans. Sierd Woudstra (Grand Rapids: Wm. B. Eerdmans, 1979), p. 90.
17. Berkouwer, *Sin*, chap. 4, "Sin and the Demonic Realm."
18. Barth, *Church Dogmatics*; Otto Weber, *Foundations of Dogmatics*, vol. 1, trans. Darrell Guder (Grand Rapids: Wm. B. Eerdmans, 1981), "The Evil One," pp. 488ff.
19. Becker, *Escape from Evil*, passim.
20. Peck, *People of the Lie*, chap. 6, "Mylai: An Examination of Evil," pp. 212–53.
21. Becker and Peck are not alone in pondering the phonomenon of mass evil. Karl Menninger has a chapter on "Sin as Collective Irresponsibility" in *Whatever Became of Sin?* pp. 94–132.
22. Vogel, *Gott in Christo*, pp. 588–90.
23. R. Knierim, *Die Hauptbegriffe für Sünde in AT* (Gütersloh: G. Mohn, 1965).
24. TDNT, s.v. "Harmantanō."
25. R.J. de Vries, IDB, s.v. "Sin, Sinners."
26. Paul Jacobs, *Evangelisches Kirchen Lexikon*, 3:1228 (numbering and italics are his).

Chapter 7. Consequences of Sin

1. See the surveys alone in B. T. Dahlberg, IDB, s.v. "Wrath of God"; Xavier Leon-Dufour, ed., *Dictionary of Biblical Theology*, s.v. "Wrath." For a very balanced theological review of the issues, see Berkhof, *Christian Faith*, pp. 126–30.
2. Cf. TDNT, s.v. "*hypodikos*."
3. Orr, *Sin as a Problem of Today* (New York and London: Hodder and Stoughton, [1910]), pp. 189ff. It is my impression that this is also G. C. Berkouwer's position in *Sin*, pp. 539ff.
4. C. E. B. Cranfield, *Romans*, 1:845.
5. For the debate among Roman Catholics on this score and the options they present, see S. Trooster, *Evolution and the Doctrine of Original Sin*, trans. John A. Ter Haar (Glen Rock, N.J.: Newman Press, 1968), pp. 23–30.
6. Althaus, *Die christliche Wahrheit*, pp. 415ff.
7. Cf. Walter Brueggemann, IDBS, s.v. "Theology of Death."
8. A good representative treatment of the subject summarizing much of what these men say is Eberhard Jüngel, *Death: The Riddle and the Mystery*, trans. Iain and Ute Nicol (Philadelphia: Westminster Press, 1974).
9. Leo Tolstoy, *The Death of Ivan Ilych and Other Stories*, trans. Aylmer Maude (New York: New American Library, 1960).
10. Ernest Becker, *The Denial of Death* (New York: Free Press, 1973).
11. Thielicke, *How the World Began*, chap. 12, "The Mystery of Death," pp. 170–84.
12. Kuyper, *Sacred Theology*, p. 421.
13. James Denney, *St. Paul's Epistle to the Romans*, vol. 2 in *The Expositor's Greek Testament* (London: Hodder and Stoughton, 1917), p. 649.
14. H. E. Ryle, *The Book of Genesis*, in *The Cambridge Bible for Schools and Colleges* (Cambridge: Cambridge University Press, 1921), p. 56.
15. See the succinct summary of the debate in *The New Schaff-Herzog Encyclopedia of Religious Knowledge*, s.v. "Infant Salvation."
16. Charles Spurgeon, "Infant Salvation," *The New Park Street and Metropolitan*

Tabernacle Pulpit Sermons (London: Passmore and Alabaster, 1862), pp. 505–515. Preached Sunday morning, 29 Sept. 1861 on the text 2 Kings 4:26.

17. Joachim Jeremias, *Die Kindertaufe in den ersten vier Jahrhunderten* (Göttingen: Vandenhoeck and Ruprecht, 1958); Kurt Aland, *Taufe und Kindertaufe* (Gütersloh: Gütersloher Verlag, 1971).

18. Calvin, *Institutes*, vol. 1, bk. 2, chaps. 1–3.

19. See note 63 on *Generalem Dei gratiam*, ibid., p. 276, and pars. 12–17 of chap. 2.

20. Kuyper defined common grace as follows: ". . . that act of God by which *negatively* He curbs the operations of Satan, death and sin, and by which *positively* He creates an intermediate state for this cosmos, as well as for our human race, which is and continues to be deeply and radically sinful, and in which sin cannot work out its end (telos)." *Principles of Sacred Theology*, trans. J. Hendrik De Vries (Grand Rapids: Wm. B. Eerdmans, 1954), p. 279. See also the summary statement by Cornelius Van Til in *Twentieth Century Encyclopedia of Religious Knowledge*, s.v. "Common Grace."

21. Cf. Robert Nisbet, *History of the Idea of Progress* (New York: Basic Books, 1980).

22. Cf. *Sacramentum Mundi*, s.v. "Progress," and EP, s.v. "The Idea of Progress."

23. Berkhof, *Christian Faith*, pp. 512–15. It must also be remarked that Nisbet in *Idea of Progress* mentions theologians of earlier epochs but does not deal with contemporary theologians.

24. Nisbet, *Idea of Progress*, pp. 317ff.

25. Interestingly, Karl Barth is on the side of the pessimists, although he believes that there may be spurts of progress as well as unanticipated reversals. *Church Dogmatics*, vol. 4, bk. 1, trans. G. W. Bromley (Edinburgh: T. and T. Clark, 1956), p. 507.

26. Houston Smith, *Forgotten Truth*, chap. 6, "Hope, Yes; Progress, No," pp. 188–45.

27. Ibid., p. 124.

28. Ibid., p. 131. Surprisingly, Smith has some good words for scientific creationists because they are the only group in America blowing the whistle on the conversion of valid scientific data into a vast evolutionary scenario that has become humanity's final philosophy or metaphysics. From Protagoras's dictum that "man is the measure of all things" has now come the modern dictum, "evolution is the measure of all things."

29. We are dealing with art for art's sake especially as it relates to censorship and open debate. In a very comprehensive survey John Hospers discusses the complexity of the subject and shows that some artists believe that the goal of art is morality (e.g., Leo Tolstoy). Cf. EB (15), s.v. "Art, Philosophy of."

30. One of the surprises (of which there are almost too many!) of Karl Barth is his interest in art, revealed in his correspondence with Carl Zuchmayer. He even calls Zuchmayer's poetry a priestly ministry. *A Late Friendship: The Letters of Karl Barth and Carl Zuchmayer*, preface Hinrich Stoevesandt, trans. Geoffrey Bromiley (Grand Rapids: Wm. B. Eerdmans, 1982), p. 13.

31. David Riesman, *The Lonely Crowd: A Study of The Changing American Character* (New Haven, Conn.: Yale University Press, 1950).

32. Cf. Eric Josephson and Mary Josephson, eds., *Man Alone: Alienation in Modern Society* (New York: Dell Publishers, 1962). Cf. also EB (15), s.v. "Alienation," and EP, s.v. "Alienation."

Chapter 8. Sin Among the Theologians

1. Schleiermacher, *Christian Faith*, secs. 66–82, pp. 271–341. Cf. also Müller, *Christian Doctrine of Sin*, 1:346–59.
2. Schleiermacher, *Christian Faith*, p. 272.
3. Ibid., p. 279.
4. Barth, *Church Dogmatics*, vol. 4, bk. 1, p. 377.
5. Rauschenbusch, *Social Gospel*, chap. 6, "The Nature of Sin," pp. 45–56.
6. Cf. W. E. Orchard's summary of Ritschl's doctrine of sin and his acerbic criticisms in *Modern Theories of Sin* (London: James Clark, 1910), pp. 79–88.
7. Rauschenbusch, *Social Gospel*, chaps. 4–9.
8. The movement in American theology known as realism (meaning a more realistic interpretation of the doctrine of sin) was a strong reaction to the superficial and optimistic characteristics of the earlier liberal theologians and Social Gospelers. It is narrated for us in Thelen, *Man As Sinner* and in H. Shelton Smith, *Changing Concepts of Original Sin*. The most thorough treatment of it is certainly Reinhold Niebuhr's *The Nature and Destiny of Man: A Christian Interpretation*, 2 vols. (New York: Charles Scribner's Sons, 1948).
9. Baumann, *Erbsünde*, pp. 248ff.
10. Brunner, *Man in Revolt*, p. 204.
11. Paul Tillich, *Systematic Theology*, vol. 2, *Existence and the Christ* (Chicago: The University of Chicago Press, 1957), pp. 29–58.
12. Barth, *Church Dogmatics*, IV/1, sec. 60, "The Pride and Fall of Man," pp. 358–513.
13. Berkhof, *Christian Faith*, p. xi.
14. Orlando E. Costas, *Christ Outside the Gate: Mission Beyond Christendom* (Maryknoll, N.Y.: Orbis Books, 1982).
15. An excellent summary of the Latin American problems is to be found in José Míguez Bonino, *Doing Theology in a Revolutionary Situation* (Philadelphia: Fortress Press, 1975).
16. Cf. Míguez Bonino, *Christians and Marxists: The Mutual Challenge to Revolution* (Grand Rapids: Wm. B. Eerdmans, 1976), and in critique, J. Andrew Kirk, *Liberation Theology: An Evangelical View from the Third World* (Atlanta: John Know Press, 1979).
17. A most interesting book is that of Thomas D. Hanks, *God So Loved the Third World: The Bible, the Reformation, and Liberation Theologies*, trans. James C. Dekker (Maryknoll, N.Y.: Orbis Books, 1983). It was written originally in Spanish by the author, whose roots are American evangelical, and it is a sturdy defense of Latin American liberation theology.

Chapter 9. Rationale for the Doctrine of Sin

1. Menninger, *Whatever Became of Sin?*, p. 46 (italics and caps are his).
2. Mowrer, *Chrisis in Psychiatry*, p. 40 (italics are his). Another psychotherapist willing to use the expression Original Sin (in Tillichian terms) is Thomas A. Harris, *I'm OK—You're OK* (New York: Avva Books, 1967), pp. 259–65.
3. MacIntyre's *After Virtue* is considered one of the modern classics in ethics, yet,

like so many texts in ethics, little is said of crime, vices, and sin. When works on ethics are this lopsided in the distribution of material they are very much like half-painted pictures.

4. Kuyper, *Sacred Theology*, pp. 106–14.
5. No writer in recent times has so emphasized the fragile character of science than Paul Feyerabend, *Against Method*.
6. HERE, s.v. "Sin" and "Fall."
7. Cf. the survey of world religions and their gospels in Aldwinckle's *Jesus—A Savior or the Savior?* Similarly in Dillistone, *Atonement*.
8. Is there such an entity as a totally degenerate tribe of people? Lewis Thomas thinks that the Iks of Uganda come close to it. The Iks are a tribe who, having been forced out of their tribal land and tribal patterns, have become a totally repulsive people. A two-year anthropological survey revealed their degeneracy. They defecate on each other's doorstep; they laugh at tragic occurrences; they are loveless; they are brutal with children; they are an ugly, contemptible people. Thomas's point is that if our own lives were so interrupted we too would become like Iks. *The Lives of a Cell: Notes of a Biology Watcher* (New York: Bantam Books, 1975), pp. 126–29.
9. Laura López, "Torture: A World Wide Epidemic," *Time*, 16 April 1984, p. 39.
10. See Berkouwer, *Sin*, chap. 9, "The Gravity and Gradation of Sin."
11. Barth, *Church Dogmatics*, col. 4, bk. 2, sec. 65, pp. 378ff.
12. Lewis, *The Great Divorce*, pp. 5–8.
13. Berkhouwer, *Sin*, pp. 546–78.

Selected Bibliography

Adams, Fred T. *The Way to Modern Man: An Introduction to Human Evolu-
tion.* New York: Teachers College Press, 1968.
Aland, Kurt. *Taufe und Kindertaufe.* Gütersloh: Gütersloher Verlag, 1971.
Aldwinckle, Russell F. *Jesus—A Savior or the Savior? Religious Pluralism in
Christian Perspective.* Macon, Ga.: Mercer University Press, 1982.
Althaus, Paul. *Die christliche Wahrheit: Lehrbuch der Dogmatik.* 5th ed. Gü-
tersloh: Carl Bertelsmann, 1959.
Barrett, C. K. *From First Adam to Last: A Study in Pauline Theology.* New
York; Charles Scribners, 1962.
Barth, Karl. *Christ and Adam: Man and Humanity in Romans 5.* Translated
by T. A. Smail. London and Edinburgh: Oliver and Boyd. 1956.
Barth, Karl. *Church Dogmatics,* 13 vols. Translated and edited by Geoffrey
Bromiley and F. F. Bruce. Edinburgh: T. and T. Clark, 1936–1969.
Barth, Karl, and Carl Zuckmayer. *A Late Friendship: The Letters of Karl Barth
and Carl Zuckmayer.* Preface by Hinrich Stoevesandt, translated
by Geoffrey Bromily. Grand Rapids: Wm. B. Eerdmans, 1982.
Baumann, Urs. *Erbsünde: Ihr traditionelles Verständnis in der Krise heutiger
Theologie.* Freiburg: Herder, 1970.
Becker, Ernest. *The Denial of Death.* New York: Free Press, 1973.
Becker, Ernest. *Escape from Evil.* New York: Free Press, 1975.
Bergson, Henri. *Creative Evolution.* Translated by Arthur Mitchell. Lon-
don: Macmillan, 1911.
Berkhof, Hendrikus. *Christian Faith.* Translated by Sierd Woudstra. Grand
Rapids: Wm. B. Eerdmans, 1979.
Berkouwer, G. C. *Sin.* Translated by Philip C. Holtrop. Grand Rapids:
Wm. B. Eerdmans, 1971.
Bromiley, Geoffrey W. *An Introduction to the Theology of Karl Barth.* Grand
Rapids: Wm. B. Eerdmans, 1979.
Brunner, Emil. *Man in Revolt: A Christian Anthropology.* Translated by Ol-
ive Wyon. Philadelphia: Westminster Press, 1947.
Calvin, John. *Institutes of the Christian Religion.* Edited by John T. McNeill;
translated by Ford Lewis Battles. Philadelphia: Westminster
Press, 1960.
Camus, Albert. *The Fall.* Translated by Justin O'Brien. New York: Alfred
A. Knopf, 1957.
Camus, Albert. *The Plague.* Translated by Stuart Gilbert. New York: Vin-
tage Books, 1948.

Camus, Albert. *The Rebel: An Essay on Man in Revolt.* Translated by Anthony Bower. New York: Vintage Books, 1956.

Camus, Albert. *The Stranger.* Translated by Stuart Gilbert. New York: Vintage Books, 1954.

Caplan, L., ed. *The Sociobiology Debate.* New York: Harper & Row, 1978.

Cassirer, Ernst. *The Philosphy of the Enlightenment.* Translated by Fritz C. A. Koelln and James P. Pettegrove. Boston: Beacon Press, 1951.

Cherbonnier, E. La B. *Hardness of Heart: A Contemporary Interpretation of the Doctrine of Sin.* Garden City, N.Y.: Doubleday, 1955.

Choron, Jacques. *Death and Western Thought.* New York: Collier Books, 1963.

Chorover, Stephen L. *From Genesis to Geonocide: The Meaning of Human Nature and the Power of Behavior Control.* Cambridge, Mass.: MIT Press, 1979.

Clark, Grahame. *World Prehistory in a New Perspective.* 3d ed. Cambridge: Cambridge University Press, 1977.

Costas, Orlando E. *Christ Outside the Gate: Mission Beyond Christendom.* Maryknoll, N.Y.: Orbis Books, 1982.

Cranfield, C. E. B. *A Critical and Exegetical Commentary on the Epistle to the Romans.* 2 vols. 6th ed. (entirely rewritten). Edinburgh: T. and T. Clark, 1975–1979.

Davidson, Robert. *Genesis 1–11: The Cambridge Bible Commentary.* Cambridge: Cambridge University Press, 1973.

De Rosa, Peter. *Christ and Original Sin.* Milwaukee: Bruce Publishing, 1967.

Denny James. *St. Paul's Epistle to the Romans. Vol 2 of The Expositor's Greek Testament.* London: Hodder and Stoughton, 1917.

Denton, David E. *The Philosophy of Albert Camus.* Boston: Prime Publishers, 1967.

Dillistone, F. W. *The Christian Understanding of Atonement.* Philadelphia: Westminster Press, 1968.

Doss, Richard W. *The Last Enemy: A Christian Understanding of Death.* San Francisco: Harper & Row, 1974.

Dostoyevsky, Fyodor. *Crime and Punishment.* Translated by Constance Garnett. New York: Random House, 1950.

Edwards, Jonathan. *The Great Christian Doctrine of Original Sin Defended. Vol 2 of The Works of President Edwards.* New York: S. Converse, 1829.

Elert, Werner. *Der christliche Glaube: Grundlinien der Luterischen Dogmatik.* 5th ed. Hamburg: Furche-Verlag, 1960.

Eliot, T. S. *The Family Reunion.* New York, Harcourt, Brace, and World, 1937.

Fairbairn, Andrew. *The Philosophy of the Christian Religion.* New York: Macmillan, 1902.

Feyerabend, Paul. *Against Method: Outline of an Anarchistic Theory of Knowledge.* London: Verso, 1975.

Ghiselin, Michael T. *The Triumph of the Darwinian Method.* Berkeley and Los Angeles: University of California Press, 1969.

Greene, John C. *The Death of Adam: Evolution and Its Impact on Western Thought.* Ames, Iowa: Iowa State University Press, 1959.

Gross, Julius. *Entstehungsgeschichte des Erbsündedogmas.* 4 vols. Munich: Ernst Reinhardt, 1960–72.

Hamidullah, Muhammad. *Introduction to Islam.* 2d ed. Paris: Centre Culturel Islamique, 1969.

Hanks, Thomas D. *God So Loved the Third World: The Bible, The Reformation, and Liberation Theologies.* Translated by James C. Dekker. Maryknoll, N.Y.: Orbis Books, 1983.

Hick, John H. *Evil and the God of Love.* Rev. ed. San Francisco: Harper & Row, 1966.

Hunsinger, George. *Karl Barth and Radical Politics.* Philadelphia: Westminster Press, 1976.

Jeremias, Joachim. *Die Kindertaufe in den ersten vier Jahrhunderten.* Göttingen: Vandenhoeck and Ruprecht, 1958.

Josephson, Eric, and Mary Josephson, ed. *Man Alone: Alienation in Modern Society.* New York: Dell Publishers, 1962.

Jüngel, Eberhard. *Death: The Riddle and the Mystery.* Translated by Iain and Ute Nicol. Philadelphia: Westminster Press, 1974.

Kant, Immanuel. *The Critique of Practical Reason and Other Writings in Moral Philosophy.* Translated and edited by Lewis White Beck. Chicago: University of Chicago Press, 1949.

Kant, Immanuel. *Religion Within the Limits of Reason Alone.* Translated by Theodore M. Greene and Hoyt H. Hudson. New York: Harper, 1960.

Kierkegaard, Søren. *The Concept of Anxiety: A Simple Psychologically Orienting Deliberation on the Dogmatic Issue of Hereditary Sin.* Edited and translated by Reidar Thomte and Albert B. Anderson. Princeton: Princeton University Press, 1980.

Kierkegaard, Søren. *Concluding Unscientific Postscript.* Translated by David F. Swenson; edited by Walter Lowrie. Princeton: Princeton University Press, 1944.

Kirk, J. Andrews. *Liberation Theology: An Evangelical View from the Third World.* Atlanta: John Knox Press, 1979.

Kreck, Walter. *Grundfragen der Dogmatik.* Munich: Chr. Kaiser Verlag, 1970.

Kuyper, Abraham. *Principles of Sacred Theology.* Translated by J. Kendrik de Vries. Grand Rapids: Wm. B. Eerdmans, 1954.

Lengsfeld, Peter. *Adam und Christus: Die Adam-Christus Typologie im Neuen Testament und ihre dogmatische Verwendung bei M.J. Scheeben und K. Barth.* Essen: Ludgerus-Verlag Hubert Wingen, 1965.

Lewis, C. S. *Christian Reflections.* Edited by Walter Hooper. Grand Rapids, Wm. B. Eerdmans, 1967.

Lewis, C. S. *The Great Divorce.* New York: Macmillan, 1946.

Lewis, C. S. *Perelandra: A Novel.* New York: Macmillan, 1944.

Lewis, C. S. *The Problem of Pain.* New York: Macmillan, 1962.

Lewis, C. S. *That Hideous Strength: A Modern Fairy-tale for Grown-ups.* New York: Macmillan, 1946.

MacIntyre, Alastair. *After Virtue: A Study in Moral Theory.* Notre Dame, Ind.: University of Notre Dame Press, 1980.

Maycock, F. H. *Original Sin.* Glasgow: Glasgow University Press, 1948.

Menniger, Karl, *Whatever Became of Sin?* New York: Hawthorn Books, 1973.

Míguez Bonino, José. *Christians and Marxists: The Mutal Challenge to Revolution.* Grand Rapids: Wm. B. Eerdmans, 1976.

Míguez Bonino, José. *Doing Theology in a Revolutionary Situation.* Philadelphia: Fortress Press, 1975.

Miller, William R., ed. *Contemporary American Protestant Thought, 1900–1970.* Indianapolis: Bobbs-Merrill, 1973.

Mowrer, O. Hobart, *The Crisis in Psychiatry and Religion.* Princeton, N.J.: D. Van Nostrand, 1961.

Moxon, Reginald Stewart. *The Doctrine of Sin: A Critical and Historical Investigation into the Views of the Concept of Sin Held in Early Christian Mediaevel, and Modern Times.* London: George Allen and Unwin, 1922.

Müller, Julius. *The Christian Doctrine of Sin.* 2 vols. Translated by William Urwick. Edinburgh: T. and T. Clark, 1885.

Murray, John. *The Imputation of Adam's Sin.* Grand Rapids: Wm. B. Eerdmans, 1959.

Nevius, John Livingston. *Demon Possession and Allied Themes.* 2d. ed. Chicago: Fleming H. Revell, 1896.

Niebuhr, Reinhold. *The Nature and Denstiny of Man: A Christian Interpretation.* 2 vols. New York: Charles Scribner's Sons, 1948.

Nisbet, Robert. *History of the Idea of Progress.* New York: Basic Books, 1979.

Orchard, W. E. *Modern Theories of Sin.* London: James Clark, 1910.

Orr, James. *The Christian View of God and the World as Centering in the Incarnation.* 1893. Reprint. Grand Rapids: Wm. B. Eerdmans, 1948.

Orr, James. *God's Image in Man and Its Defacement in the Light of Modern Denials.* Grand Rapids: Wm. B. Eerdmans, [1905].

Orr, James. *Sin as a Problem of Today.* New York and London: Hodder and Stoughton, [1910].

Ott, Heinrich, ed. *Die Antwort des Glaubens: Systematische Theologie in 50 Artikeln.* Berlin: Kreuz-Verlag, 1972.

Pascal, Blaise. *Pensées.* Translated by A. J. Krailsheimer. Edited by Louis Lafuma. New York: Penguin Books.

Peck, M. Scott. *People of the Lie: The Hope for Healing Human Evil.* New York: Simon and Schuster, 1983.

Peck, M. Scott. *The Road Less Traveled: A New Psychology of Love, Traditional Values and Spiritual Growth.* New York: Simon and Schuster, 1978.

Plantinga, Alvin. *God, Freedom, and Evil.* New York: Harper & Row, 1974.

Prenter, Regin. *Schöpfung und Erlösung: Dogmatik.* 2 vols. Translated from Danish by Christiane Boehncke-Sjöberg. Göttingen: Vandenhoeck and Ruprecht, 1958–60.

Quasten, Johannes. *Patrology.* Vol. 2, *The Ante-Nicene Literature after Irenaeus.* Westminster, Maryland: Newman Press, 1953.

Ramm, Bernard. *The Devil, Seven Wormwoods, and God.* Waco, Texas: Word Books, 1977.

Renckens, Henricus. *Israel's Concept of the Beginning: The Theology of Genesis I–III.* Translated by Charles Napier. New York: Herder and Herder, 1964.

Rhinelander, Philip H. *Is Man Incomprehensible to Man?* New York: W. H. Freeman, 1974.

Rich, Arthur. *Pascals Bild vom Menschen: Eine Studie über die Dialelctik von Natur und Gnade in den "Pensées."* Zürich: Zwingli-Verlag, 1953.

Ridderbos, Herman. *Paul: An Outline of His Theology.* Translated by John Richard de Witt. Grand Rapids: Wm. B. Eerdmans, 1975.

Riesman, David. *The Lonely Crowd: A Study of the Changing American Character.* New Haven, Conn: Yale University Press, 1950.

Robinson, H. Wheeler. *Corporate Personality in Ancient Israel.* Rev. ed. Edited by Gene M. Tucker. Philadelphia: Fortress Press, 1980.

Rondet, Henri. *Original Sin: The Patristic and Theological Background.* Translated by Cajetan Finegan. Staten Island, New York: Alba House, 1972.

Ryle, H. E. *The Book of Genesis in The Cambridge Bible for Schools and Colleges.* Cambridge: Cambridge University Press, 1921.

Samenow, Stanton E. *Inside the Criminal Mind.* New York: Times Books, 1984.

Scharbert, Josef. *Prolegomena eines Alttestamentlers zur Erbsündenlehre.* Vol. 37 of *Quaestiones Disputatae.* Freiburg: Herder, 1968.

Schleiermacher, Friedrich. *The Christian Faith.* Translated from 2d German ed. by H. R. MacKintosh and J. S. Stewart. Edinburgh: T. and T. Clark, 1928.

Skinner, B.F. *Beyond Freedom and Dignity.* New York: Bantam Books, 1972.

Skinner, B.F. *Walden Two.* New York: Macmillan, 1948.

Skinner, John, *A Critical and Exegetical Commentary on Genesis.* 2d ed. Vol 1 of *The International Critical Commentary.* Edinburgh: T. and T. Clark, 1930.

Smith, H. Shelton. *Changing Concepts of Original Sin: A Study in American Theology Since 1750.* New York: Charles Schribner's Sons, 1955.

Smith, Huston. *Beyond the Post-Modern Mind.* New York: Crossroad, 1982.

Smith, Huston. *Forgotten Truth: The Primordial Tradition.* New York: Harper & Row, 1976.

Speiser, E. A., ed. *Genesis.* Vol. 1 of *The Anchor Bible.* Garden City, N.Y.: Doubleday, 1982.

Spurgeon, Charles. "Infant Salvation." In *The New Park Street and Metropolitan Tabernacle Pulpit Sermons,* pp. 505–515. London: Passmore and Alabaster, 1862.

Tennant, Frederick R. *The Concept of Sin.* Cambridge: Cambridge University Press, 1912.

Tennant, Frederick R. *The Origin and Propagation of Sin: Being the Hulsean Lectures Delivered Before the University of Cambridge in 1901–2.* 2d ed. Cambridge: Cambridge University Press, 1908.

Tennant, Frederick R. *The Sources of the Doctrines of the Fall and Original Sin.* 1903. Reprint. New York: Schocken Books, 1968.

Thelen, Mary Frances. *Man as Sinner in Contemporary American Realistic Theology.* New York: King's Crown Press, 1946.

Thielicke, Helmut. *How the World Began: Man in the First Chapters of the Bible.* Translated by John W. Doberstein. Philadelphia: Muhlenberg Press, 1961.

Thomas, Lewis. *The Lives of a Cell: Notes of a Biology Watcher.* New York: Bantam Books, 1975.

Tillich, Paul. *Systematic Theology.* Vol. 2, *Existence and the Christ.* Chicago: University of Chicago Press, 1957.

Tolstoy, Leo. *The Death of Ivan Ilych and Other Stores.* Translated by Aylmer Maude. New York: New American Library, 1960.

Trillhaas, Wolfgang. *Dogmatick.* Berlin: Alfred Töpelmann, 1962.

Trooster, S. *Evolution and the Doctrine of Original Sin.* Translated by John A. Ter Haar. Glen Rock, N.J.: Newman Press, 1968.

Unamuno, Miguel de. *The Tragic Sense of Life in Men and in Peoples.* Translated by J. E. Crawford Flitch. New York: Dover Publications, 1945.

Vawter, Bruce. *On Genesis: A New Reading.* Garden City, N.Y.: Doubleday, 1977.

Vogel, Heinrich. *Gott in Christo: Ein Erkenntnisgang durch die Grundprobleme der Dogmatik.* 2d ed. Berlin: Lettner Verlag, 1952.

Voltaire. *Candide, Zadig and Selected Stories.* Translated by Donald M. Frame. New York: New American Library, 1961.

Warfield, Benjamin B. *Studies in Tertullian and Augustine.* New York: Oxford University Press, 1930.

Weger, Karl-Heinz. *Theologie der Erbsünde.* Freiburg: Herder, 1970.

Westermann, Claus. *Creation.* Translated by John J. Scullion. Philadelphia: Fortress Press, 1974.

White, Andrew D. *A History of the Warfare of Science with Theology in Christendom.* 2 vols. New York: D. Appleton, 1896.

Williams, Norman Powell. *The Ideas of the Fall and Original Sin: A Historical and Critical Study.* London: Longmans, Green, and Co., 1927.

Wilson, Edward O. *Sociobiology: The New Synthesis.* Cambridge: Harvard University Press, 1975.

Wolff, Hans Walter. *Anthropology of the Old Testament.* Translated by Margaret Kohl. Philadelphia: Fortress Press, 1974.

Index